Roger Bede Vaughan

Science and Religion

Lectures on the Reasonableness of Christianity

Roger Bede Vaughan

Science and Religion
Lectures on the Reasonableness of Christianity

ISBN/EAN: 9783337027926

Printed in Europe, USA, Canada, Australia, Japan

Cover: Foto ©Lupo / pixelio.de

More available books at **www.hansebooks.com**

LECTURES

— ON THE —

Reasonableness of Christianity and the Shallowness of Unbelief.

DELIVERED BY THE

MOST REV. ROGER BEDE VAUGHAN,

ARCHBISHOP OF SYDNEY.

MAN!   GOD!   DENIAL!   FAITH!

BALTIMORE:
JOHN B. PIET.
1879.

JOHN B. PIET,
PRINTER AND PUBLISHER.

To

The Right Reverend

WILLIAM BERNARD ULLATHORNE, D.D., O.S.B.,

Bishop of Birmingham.

My Dear Lord—

Allow me to connect your name—a name still held in benediction in Australia—with these Arguments of mine in support of Christianity. I ask you for this favor, because I feel it a very pleasant thing, living here, so far away from old ties and old friends, to associate myself and my work with the name of one who did so much in his day for the Australian Church; and, who, still, I have reason to believe, looks back with interest upon a field in which he sowed a seed the fruits of which younger men are gathering.

Believe me, my Dear Lord, ever to be,
With much reverence,
Your affectionate Confrère,

† ROGER BEDE,
Archbishop of Sydney.

Sydney, May, 1879.

On the 9th of March, 1879, his Grace, the Most Rev. Archbishop Vaughan, began a course of Lenten lectures in his pro-Cathedral in Sydney, Australia. The congregations which assembled to hear him on that and the four succeeding Sundays were immense, and were composed of Protestants and infidels, as well as Catholics. On the conclusion of the series, the Archbishop was urgently requested to publish his discourses, and, after considerable importuning, he consented. They are now reprinted for the benefit of American readers, and are herewith offered as most opportune and powerful to the attention of Christians of all denominations, and to all other men of good will, who lost in the slough of doubt, yet long for the solid ground of certainty and truth.

INTRODUCTORY ADDRESS.

It is my purpose during the four next Sunday evenings to develop four arguments touching the reasonableness of Christianity and the shallowness of Unbelief. I purpose to show that the Religion of Denial is not only a shallow one, but also that it cannot be made to work; and that, on the other hand, the religion of Affirmation, or, in other words, Christianity, is adapted in a marvellous manner to the wants of humanity, and is supported by such an array of arguments, by so weighty a cumulus of probabilities, is so consonant to reason, that to reject it would be to act not only against the enlightened dictates of conscience, but also in opposition to those universally accepted maxims of prudence which are the guide of all reasonable men in every important secular affair of life. I hope to bring out clearly before you, from the intellectual and moral constitution of man, evidences of his having been made for something beyond merely living as an animal upon the earth; I hope to show, from what we know of the Deity, from the arguments and evidences which we possess, and which lie spread before the intellectual eye of every thinking rational creature regarding His providence and governance of human things, that His existence is as undeniable a fact as the existence of man himself, and that before the creature can deny the existence of his Maker, he must first of all deny the truthfulness of those intellectual and moral faculties which, for the very initial steps of reasoning, he cannot choose but trust. I hope to show you that, when the arguments and evidences which prove that man was made for a better and a higher life than this are brought into comparison with the proofs we possess of an overruling Providence of God, the result is so harmonious as to furnish an additional reason for our belief in the high destiny of man, and in the loving mercy of a Personal God.

It will be my aim, moreover, to demonstrate, for that, at all events, is capable of absolute demonstration, that the Religion of Denial, or Unbelief, is not merely shallow as a philosophy and empty as a religion, but, moreover, that it is the fruitful parent, like the plague or the small-pox in the physical order, of intellectual imbecility, moral depravity and spiritual death. And, finally, having called your attention to the awful consequences of unbelief; to its infantine incapacity for doing anything for suffering and sinning humanity, morally or spiritually; to the extreme vanity and emptiness of its pretensions; to the darknesses and difficulties it creates, without being able to solve the most vital problems; having endeavored to knock that hideous idol from its pedestal, I shall then proceed to unfold to you the supreme advantages of the Religion of Christianity, to show you how it, as no other system has ever done, solves difficulties, unravels doubts, gives a meaning to life and an illumination to death; and that every faculty of man, moral and intellectual, loudly proclaims that, though like all things else, it is surrounded by obscurities, and is charged with mysteries, that is to say, things which during this life cannot be explained away, still, its bases are so wide and deep, its proofs so multitudinous, and, when taken together, so overwhelming, compared with the best arguments for any other system, that enlightened reason in the order of thought, and human prudence in the practical order, compel men, in spite of all its difficulties, which are in them rather than in it, to submit to its authority.

And whilst I purpose to carry out this programme, I am deeply sensible of the difficulty of the undertaking. Not that I am conscious of a shadow of doubt as to the overwhelming character of the arguments by which the position I have assumed can be supported. I have a most perfect confidence in my cause; but my great difficulty is myself. Supposing there were in existence some powerful being who assured me that he would bestow upon me adequate capacity for drawing out before you, in their full number and in all their force, the proofs in favor of my thesis, then I should simply walk in triumph over the field; then the opponents of Positive Religion would at once, and with reply impossible, be simply and irrevocably overwhelmed. But such is not the case. I feel that I have far more to say than I shall ever be able to hint at; that the few proofs and evidences that I shall be able to make use of might be urged with ten thousand times more vigor than I shall be able to bring to bear; and that I am intellectually incapable, however much pains I may take, of drawing out intelligibly before you one-tenth of the proofs and consequences which go to make up the one grand argument for Christianity. All this I feel with great oppressiveness; and it makes me conscious of a sort of dread of embarking upon so perilous an intellectual voyage. Yet, on the other hand, I cannot help thinking that if Christianity is what we know it to be, a giant of enormous force and immense proportions, that if I am enabled to draw out before you some kind of rough, imperfect sketch even of that giant's foot or finger, you will be able to give more than a reasonable guess as to the nature and characteristics of that being to whom that foot or finger belongs. It is not necessary, fortunately, in order to convince a reasonable man, to bring to bear upon him every possible argument in favor of a given proposition. Sufficient proof is enough proof, and enough proof is that which would satisfy a man of good will, and one who *sciens et prudens*, and without bias, makes use of the head that God has given him. Again: As a rule, what convinces one reasonable man will generally convince another reasonable man. If I myself so deeply believe in Christianity as to be ready to die for it, should God give me the grace, rather than deny it; if I, a man, with intellect and reason like other men, am so certain about it, so positive, surely, I say to myself, I must have very good reasons for being so. I am not a Christian by caprice. I may have been born one; traditions of Christianity may have biassed me with their power; still, have I not studied the Christian scheme from the standpoint of reason? Have I not analyzed it and weighed it, and compared it with other schemes, and with the doctrines of those who call themselves philosophers of an enlightened age, and with the advanced teaching of modern science and progressive infidelity?

And is it not a fact, I say to myself, that the more I study these, the less inclined I feel to trust my soul and my salvation and my future, whatever it may be, to them? Is it not a fact that they offer me stones for bread, and give neither to my moral nor my intellectual nor to my spiritual nature the slightest satisfaction? Do I not find their arguments shallow, their theories impracticable, and their talk fit at best only for the closet; or for men who are as ignorant as children of the actualities of life, and of the wants and yearnings of striving humanity? Are they not men who do not look at the concrete world as it is, and at its practical wants; and who appear incapable of weighing those deep arguments of the heart and of the conscience, which are as legitimate and as urgent as any syllogism in philosophy? Why, then, if I feel and know these things, cannot I impart my reasons for so feeling and so knowing to others? Surely, what so fully satisfies me will satisfy at least many amongst them; and, if I feel the deepest consolation and rest in the Christian philosophy and religion, they also, could I impart my reasons to them for doing so, would feel consolation and rest in them also. Thus, these two simple facts, that reason sufficient is reason enough, and that what affects me will, in all probability, affect many others in the same way, have led me to make the venture of these lectures, and to do what in me lies to impart to others, if it be possible, some of those reasons and evidences which have the effect of giving such rest and such solace, not only to me, but to millions of others who have learnt the true intellectual wisdom of subjecting their reasons to to the obedience of faith.

Yet, though I am venturing on these expositions of the Christian position, still I do not venture to address myself to all men indiscriminately. I confine myself to two classes —to those who, though they are firm believers, will be glad to inspect some of those evidences which make up the vestibule leading to the realms of supernatural faith; and to those who are " men of good will," who are anxious to know the truth, and willing. when they know it, to embrace it. I do not pretend to address myself to wranglers or to rhetoricians, nor to those whose lives are dedicated to the excitement of intellectual.combats. It is to the serious, the thoughtful, the earnest, to those who cannot help feeling that, after all, life means more than eating and drinking and making money; that they have within them, and seem to perceive outside them, a something, a witness or a voice, which speaks, or seems to speak, of another state of being and another world than this; and who would be glad to learn what can be said in favor of the great fundamental positions of the Christian system. There are thousands of such as these in every big city here and abroad; thousands of men and women, young and old, who are hungering for bread, with none to break it to them; thousands who are haunted by a doubt and misgiving which they do not know how to rid themselves of, but which a little light would solve and dissipate; thousands who, for want of such light, lead miserable, degraded lives, or, at best, blighted and useless ones; and who, had they the illumination and the grace, would be lifted up above themselves, and find that they were not made in vain; and would learn, to their intense relief of mind and heart, that a great destiny was opened out before them, which would give a nobility and purpose to human life, which, without these, is a dreary and almost unbearable monotony. They would become convinced—

> That nothing walks with aimless feet;
> That not one life shall be destroy'd
> Or cast as rubbish to the void,
> When God hath made the pile complete.

> That not a worm is cloven in vain;
> That not a moth, with vain desire,
> Is shrivel'd in a fruitless fire,
> Or but subserves another's gain.

Again, I am addressing myself to those actually before me, that is, to living men and women, not to the dead; not to a coming generation, but to those here present, energizing in the flesh, who have already gone through so many years of life, and are capable of seizing the principal bearings of the arguments with which I deal, and which are addressed individually to them. I am speaking to men and women who are busily engaged in the affairs of active life, and have had a fair ordinary education, and are anxious to know what they really are, where they are going, and what guide, for guide assuredly they must have, they are in duty bound to follow. I am speaking to my fellow-men, who, like myself, feel that nothing is nearly so intensely interesting as the question regarding our own future; and who are naturally anxious, as every seriously thinking man is bound to be, to understand, as far as possible, the meaning and significance of human life and moral responsibility.

But before I enter upon the four arguments which touch upon the reasonableness of Christianity and the shallowness of Unbelief, it will be well, in this introductory address, to explain for the sake of clearness, the meaning which I attach to my terms.

By Christianity, then, I mean the whole complexus of natural and supernatural religion as revealed by God in the conscience, in nature and in supernatural revelation, having a continuous history, producing on a large scale certain vast effects in the spiritual, intellectual, and moral order; whilst holding out to fallen men, as the reward of obedience, and through the death of the Son of God, the eternal happiness of heaven. By Christianity, as expressed in scientific form, I mean the *Summa* of St. Thomas of Aquin, who, with the most exact scientific precision, drew out, as upon a map, the dealings of God with man, and the relation of man to God, from the days of the first parents in the first Paradise to that day when all flesh shall see the judgment of God. I mean by Chrisrianity that force in the world of which Mr. Gladstone speaks when he says that "the Christian thought, the Christian tradition, the Christian society, are the great, the imperial thought, tradition, and society of this earth." "It is from Christendom outwards," he continues, "that power and influence radiate, not towards it and into that they flow. There seems to be one point at least on the surface of the earth, namely, among the negro races of West Africa, where Mahometanism gains ground upon Christianity; but that assuredly is not the seat of government whence will issue the *fiats* of the future, to direct the destinies of mankind." And, to be more explicit still, by Christianity I mean not broken fragmentary Christianity; I mean Christianity full and complete in all its organs, and healthy in all its frame. The only Christianity which, in my humble conviction, is thoroughly reasonable, that stands any chance of resisting the shock of modern unbelief, is the strongest and most elastic form of it—the Christianity of the Catholic Church. It alone, so far as I can see, and so far as unbelievers testify to any religion at all, will stand when the flood has swept all other forms away. So pressing, and with such volume, will the current flow, that only the firmest and the most vital organism will remain above the waters; and she, who so often has been compared to the Ark, will, it may be in some future distant day, as a great writer has already prophesied, be the only spiritual refuge left for the human family. But to confine myself to facts, and to leave forecastings alone; I say, then, it is but natural, it is but prudent, when I am encountering so formidable an athlete as Unbelief, to meet him with my most experienced and most formidable swordsman : it is but natural that I should send forward to the forefront, not the maimed or the cripple, but one who, above all the rest, in power, in past achievements, in daring, in coolness, in intellectual and moral force, in logic, in love and in discipline, stands pre-eminently first. Think not that I am carried away with prejudice, and am confounding the strong with the weak; or that I am willing to sacrifice or jeopardize the battle for the sake of a false measure or a foolish predilection. Think not that I am so vain as to indulge in empty rhetoric.

Speaking of the Pope, for whom he professes scant love, Mr. Gladstone writes, in reference to the unapproachable discipline in the Catholic Church, to this effect, he says: "The Christian community under him (that is to say, under the successor of St. Peter) is organized like an army, in which each order is in strict subjection to every order that is above it. A thousand Bishops are its generals; some two hundred thousand clergy are its subordinate officers; the laity are its proletarians. The auxiliary forces of this great military establishment are the monastic orders. And they differ from the auxiliaries of other armies in that they have a yet stricter discipline, and a more complete dependence on the head than the ordinary soldiery." . . "To the charm of an unbroken continuity," he continues, " to the majesty of an immense mass, to the energy of a closely serried organization," the Catholic Church, "adds another and a more legitimate source of strength. It undeniably contains within itself a large portion of the individual life of Christendom. The faith, the hope, the charity, which it was the office of the Gospel to engender, flourish within this precinct in the hearts of millions upon millions. . . . Many beautiful and many noble characters grow up within it. Moreover, the babes and sucklings of the Gospel, the poor, the weak, the uninstructed, the simple souls who in tranquil spheres give their heart and will to God, and whose shaded path is not scorched by the burning questions of human thought and life, these persons are probably in the Roman Church by no means worse than they would be under other Christian systems. They swell the mass of the main body, obey the word of command when it reaches them, and they help to supply the resources by which a vast machinery is kept in motion."

And, as if to confirm what I have said regarding the superior strength of Catholic Christianity, and its higher capabilities for confronting the infidelity of the day, the same distinguished statesman continues: "Yet once more. The Papal host has reason to congratulate itself on the compliments it receives from its extremest opponents, when they are contrasted with the scorn which those opponents feel for all that lies between." He says that E. Von Hartmann, the chief living oracle of German Pantheism, whilst reserving his most severe denunciations for "Liberal Protestantism," says that the Catholic Church "ought to feel flattered by his recognizing in it the legitimate champion of historical Christianity. Such, then, is the testimony given by one of our ablest English minds, and by the great German philosopher, as to the fitness of the Catholic Church, when, compared with other forms of Christianity, for stepping forward and meeting the infidelity of the age. By Christianity I mean, then, finally, "the legitimate champion of historical Christianity;" that is to say, the holy Roman Catholic and Apostolic Church.

In the next place, what do I mean by reasonableness? By reasonableness I mean that to which a man, with all his faculties in a sound condition, and using common prudence, assents, as being, under the circumstances of the case, satisfactory to his mind. I say a man, with "all his faculties in a sound condition," and not simply a man with "right reason"; for man is not merely a logical machine; logic-chopping will not carry anyone very far.

Truth appeals in different ways to the whole man, and acts upon and influences man, not merely as one possessing the gift of drawing conclusions, but as a man, just as God has made him—with his heart and head and senses. A pure heart is as much a part of a genuine man as a clear intellect, and often the heart possesses a subtlety, especially if it has been carefully trained, which spontaneously bears towards truth, when the intellect seems to see but little, and which detects fallacies and falsehoods which the reason only finds out after the heart has given the alarm. "Blessed are the clean of heart, for they shall see God," possesses a deep philosophical significance, as well as the deep lament uttered in the words: "With desolation is the whole world made desolate, because no man thinketh in his heart." When I say, then, that I am about to touch upon the reasonableness of Christianity, in its "legitimate historical exponent," I wish to signify that I hope to show that after Christianity has been weighed, and has been brought to bear upon a man as a man, that such a man will declare that it, and it alone, of all the claimants to his allegiance, considering the mystery of our being, and though it does not profess to make all things plain, legitimately challenges his assent to its dictates and its claims as the only practically prudent course open to him. Of course this is putting things on their lowest grounds; I am not denying that Christianity is capable of absolute demonstration, but I elect, in these arguments, to confine myself to proving that which is necessary for my purpose, and shall be content with defending so much ground as will carry the superstructure that I propose to build upon it.

What do I mean by Unbelief? By unbelief I mean to denote what is called the Negative School; that is to say, those various forms of unbelief which reject not merely supernatural, but also natural religion. This school includes those who call themselves "advanced thinkers" and "men of science"; it denies or ignores, as incapable of being known, the existence of God, the immortality and spirituality of the soul, free will and a future state; it declares man to be merely a cleverer kind of animal than the rest of his fellow-brutes. His horizon is bounded by the earth, and having spun out his earthly energies, he ceases absolutely to be. This life is the begin-all and the end-all for him. Of course, there are many and various gradations in this school, but the description which I have given is a sufficiently accurate sketch to serve the purpose I have in view.

Such, then, is what I mean by Unbelief. And now you might possibly ask me why I am grappling with this extreme form of infidelity. My reason is this: because that form represents the force and substance of the evils and errors with which I have to contend. As I pick out my most dexterous swordsman on the one side, so I wish to pick out the strongest on the other. If the enemy has to be encountered at all, he had best be encountered in his stronghold. If the Negative School can be shown to be a shallow one, then my task, as far as infidelity is concerned, is accomplished. Once believe in God, in man's future destiny, in the sanction of divine law, in the immortality of the soul, and, if you are logical, you must of necessity finally join the Catholic Church. Hartmann was talking sense when he said that he "treated with scorn"—the scorn merely of logic, I hope—"all that lies between Unbelief and Catholicity."

And, finally, what do I mean by shallowness, which I ascribe to the various teachings of Unbelief which are especial to the Negative School? I call that shallow which has no depth, which promises far more than it performs, and which, when tested, is found wanting. Thus, the Negative School is shallow as a philosophy, as a morality, and as a religion. It is absolutely incapable of satisfying, or even tending to satisfy, the cravings of humanity in those three most important relations. It promises that it will not merely take and fill the place of faith, that it will not only satisfy the intellect and heart equally as well as Christianity, but it pretends to be a vast improvement on Christianity, and to do far more for mankind than the Christian scheme has ever done. And whilst it makes all these rash and empty boasts, it leaves man stripped and naked, robbed of his priceless inheritance of Christian faith and hope and love. The Pantheism of Hartmann, the worship of the universe, substituted by Strauss for God, and the worship of humanity, which is proposed by Comte —all these various figments are thin and shallow inventions, the creations, no doubt, of ingenious men, but of philosophers who could not have probed the depths of humanity, and did not understand the aspirations of the heart. Or, to throw my thought into another form, and to use the language of a great master of the English tongue: "As in wines, it is one question what mode of compositions will produce a commodity drinkable in the country of origin, and what further provision may be requisite in order that the product may bear a sea voyage without turning into vinegar, so, in the matter of belief, select individuals may subsist on a poor, thin, sodden and attenuated diet, which would simply starve the multitude. Schemes, then, may suffice for the moral wants of a few intellectual and cultivated men [?], which cannot be propagated, and cannot be transmitted; which cannot bear the wear and tear of constant re-delivery; which cannot meet the countless and ever-shifting exigencies of our nature taken at large; which cannot do the rough work of the world. The colors that will endure through the term of a butterfly's existence would not avail to carry the work of Titian down from generation to generation, and century to century. Think of the twelve Agnostics, or twelve Pantheists, or twelve Materialists, setting out from some modern Jerusalem to do the work of the twelve Apostles!"

So far for the explanation of terms. The next thing to do is to define my starting point and my position. To attempt to reason with an opponent without first determining points of agreement, without carefully marking out the *locus standi*, or common ground from which to argue, is little better than beating the air and throwing up the dust.

But before I do this, I think it well, for the sake of clearness, to premise the following remark, namely, that the main current of unbelief in the present age seems to spring from the direction of what is called "Natural Science," and from scientific men whose especial study is "Nature" and her operations, but who, not content with the results of observation in their own peculiar sphere, are ever hankering after arguments from it to disprove those fundamental positions of Christianity upon which our faith so much depends. The very fact of physical science being supposed to be an antagonist to traditional beliefs, makes it all the more popular with those who are ever in search of change and intellectual excitement, and it is curious to observe how those who, in matters of religion and morality, are most severe in their verification of proofs, when there is a question of some scientific discovery upsetting some time-honored teaching of religion, are the very ones to accept, without the smallest difficulty, suppositions and hypotheses which have scarcely a shred of argument in their support. Thus there seems to be a subtle tendency in the mind of the present age towards infidelity—a secret lurking in the heart after pretexts for getting rid of a morality or religion which is a restraint on passion, curbs pride, and keeps man humble. And when to this tendency we add the fuel which is freely ministered to the fire by many of the leading physicists of the day, whose brilliancy of style or imagination captivates the vulgar, who are absolutely incapable of judging on scientific subjects, when the learned lead the ignorant into the highways of unbelief, then, of course, we cannot but expect a powerful growth in the direction of doubt or incredulity, which paralyzes the moral nature, and then, of absolute denial, which is its death. Did scientific men—men, that is, whose lives are dedicated to the investigation of nature—keep to their science, and were they content with what can be demonstrated and verified by it, then they would be looked upon by the Church as amongst the benefactors of mankind. But even scientific men are men of like passions and proclivities with their fellows, and many of them, not content with the study of "Nature," feel an indescribable itching to bring their hypotheses to bear against the teachings of religion.

The telescope may search the heavens, and it will find no God, and the scapel may enter the brain, and it will find no soul. Is God, then, a fixed star, and is the soul of man a material substance? Is it not an attribute of the Almighty that He is invisible to the carnal eye of man as at present illuminated? and is it not a characteristic of the soul that it cannot be struck with a knife or separated by a saw, however fine the teeth? Is it not our contention that the soul is immaterial, and that it cannot be handled and pulled about and dissected by coarse human hands and instruments? It will be my endeavor, then, to point out the limits of science, and to show that, so far as science teaches anything, it points steadily towards the teachings of religion; and though it is not the province of science to prove the truths of faith, still the more it is investigated and interrogated, so much the more does it, taken as a whole, in all its various branches, tend towards confirming those dictates of conscience and of reason which are the most precious guides of man upon the earth. In dealing, then, with unbelief, and unbelief especially generated by a false idea of the legitimate position and teaching of science, I start with the declaration of this incontrovertible fact, viz., that science, which undertakes to prove and verify everything, and charges religion with taking things for granted, cannot make one initial step in advance without taking for granted, and as incapable of proof, many most important and, indeed, essential propositions. The most severe scientific man, who will have his demonstration for everything, has, after all his boasting, to humble himself like a child, and to admit that unless he took as self-evident and indemonstrably certain fundamental propositions, he would not be able to lay the first stone of his scientific structure.

Allow me, in proof of this, to quote the words of one of the foremost leaders of the Negative School, Mr. Herbert Spencer. He says, speaking of experimentalism: "Throughout its argument there runs the tacit assumption that there may be a philosophy in which nothing is asserted but what is proved. It proposes to admit into the coherent fabric of its conclusions no conclusion that is incapable of being established by evidence, and thus it takes for granted that not only may all derivative truths be proved, but, also, that proof may be given of the truths from which they are derived, down to the very deepest. The consequence of this refusal to recognize some fundamental unproved truth is that its fabric of conclusions is left without a base. Giving proof of any especial proposition is assimilating it to some class of propositions known to be true. If any doubt arises respecting the general proposition cited in justification of this especial proposition, the course is to show that this general proposition is deducible from a proposition of still greater generality; and if pressed for proof of such still more general proposition, the only resource is to repeat the process. Is this process endless? If so, nothing can be proved; the whole series of propositions depends on some unassignable proposition. Has the process an end? If so, there must eventually be reached a widest proposition, one which cannot be justified by showing that it is included in any wider, one which cannot be proved. Or, to put the argument otherwise, every inference depends on premises; every premise, if it admits of proof, depends on other premises; and if the proof of the proof be continually demanded, it must either end in an unproved premise, or in the acknowledgment that there cannot be reached any premise on which the entire series of proofs depends. Hence philosophy, if it does not avowedly stand on some datum underlying reason, must acknowledge that it has nothing on which to stand, must confess itself to be baseless." ("Psychology," vol ii, p. 391.)

That Christian philosophy is at one with the Negative philosopher on this point is clear from these words of the great Catholic Spanish thinker, Balmes. He says: "Not only are not all things demonstrated, but it may even be demonstrated that some things are indemonstrable. Demonstration is a ratiocination in which we infer from evident propositions a proposition evidently connected with them. If the premises are of themselves evident, they do not admit of demonstration; if we suppose them in their turn demonstrable, we shall have the same difficulty with respect to those on which the new demonstration is founded; therefore, we must either stop at an indemonstrable point, or proceed infinitely, which would be never to finish the demonstration." ("Fundamental Philosophy," vol i, p. 106.)

Now I think that we cannot impress upon our minds too forcibly this fundamental truth, which all are obliged to assume before they begin to reason at all, that they must begin by taking the ground they stand upon for granted. Huxley and Darwin and Hartmann are here on the same level with Suarez and St. Thomas. Science does not mean a course of universal verification or demonstration; it means, at most, embracing the first truths that God has given you, and then, with such an intellect as you possess, learning how to name and catalogue and detect the mutual relations of things that are created on the earth. The fact that all demonstration or proof implies the taking for granted something that cannot be proved, the fact that all our scientific and advanced thinkers are bound as firmly by this law as the most devout Catholic, tends towards reducing their pretensions to proper proportions, and towards dispelling that cloud of mystery and that kind of absurd reverential awe with which the vulgar mind surrounds them. The proud, imperious mind of man must, before he wields his logic, submit himself to the light God has placed within him, and admit that that light is far more luminous than all the astuteness and cunning of his intellect. For, to take for granted does not mean to accept blindly; but it means that the first truths are so evident in themselves, so clear, shine with so bright an internal light, that the reason, or intellect, or conscience, if it be not altogether twisted, is compelled to accept them. The most haughty man of science, equally with the humble recluse, is bound to accept without question, without hesitation, not some particular light of his own invention, but that light in his reason and conscience, and no other, which the Almighty God has given him. Thus we possess a *locus standi*. We are one and all bound to start like little children, the proudest philosopher with the poorest peasant; and gratefully and humbly, and without question, accepting the light given us by our Heavenly Father, we make use of it in investigating Nature and for seeing just so far, and only so far, as the nature and character of that light will allow us to see.

Each man is limited by his light. No man can see beyond his light, and when he pretends to see beyond, he is merely as a blind man groping out of light into darkness; as one who is led more by the imagination of what he wishes than by the vision of what he sees. There is a profound meaning in the words of our greatest living poet when he exclaims:

> " We have but faith, we cannot know,
> For knowledge is of things we see;
> And yet we trust it comes from Thee,
> A beam in darkness let it grow."

In fact, if Christianity be true, those very postulates and positions which men even of the most transcendent genius cannot escape, must, in our present state, necessarily exist. Laborious investigation of Nature may and does result in many interesting and useful discoveries; but with all his labor, man must still submit. His best knowledge is "a beam in darkness." Or to turn from the poet to the philosopher, "The greater the circle of light," says the author of "The Unseen Universe," "the greater the circumference of darkness, and the mystery which has been driven before us looms in the darkness that surrounds this circle, growing more mysterious and more tremendous as the circumference increases. In fine, we have already remarked that the position of the scientific man is to clear a space before him from which there shall be nothing but matter and certain definite laws which he can comprehend. There are, however, three great mysteries (a trinity of mysteries) which elude, and will forever elude, his grasp, and these will persistently hover around the border of this cleared and illuminated circle; they are the mystery of matter, the mystery of life, and the mystery of God."

Thus theologian and philosopher have to take for granted their first principles, humbly and without question, and to be guided by that light, and by no other, that is accorded to them. They are forced to admit, and they do so all the more readily and emphatically in proportion as they advance in the study of their respective sciences, that what they do know is infinitesimal compared with that vast world of being that they do not know; and imperfect, or at least exceedingly obscure compared with the knowledge that might be possessed by intellects far more piercing and grasping than man's. In fact, the mysteries that present themselves at every turn in nature, and the more the more it is investigated, are perhaps in some ways more startling, and possibly more numerous than those which belong to the higher regions of religion. Both Nature and Grace seem to point to some infinite Being, all-wise and all-powerful, whose every manifestation to His creatures has upon it the countersign of His divine Perfection, pointing to the infinite attributes of the Creator, and the finite and microscopic faculties of man.

Such being the limitations of theological and scientific knowledge, founded in the greatness of God and the littleness of man, in the difference between the Infinite and the finite, it now remains for me to indicate the principal truths which, before we begin to argue, both science and religion are compelled to take for granted.

When I enter into myself, and study my own being and nature as a man, the first thing that impresses me with the irresistable force of its absolute certainty is the important fact that I am, that I exist, and am what I know and feel myself to be. Starting 'with this absolute conviction of my own existence, I examine the character and action of my own mind. I know I require no proof of it, it is with me before all proof, that I have an intellect, a will and senses, and the power of loving with my whole being. I am absolutely conscious that this intellect is my intellect, and this will my will, and this power of affection something belonging to me. This "me" I know without any demonstration; this self of mine is, as it were, the possessor of these faculties and powers: and, in the exercise of them, I am conscious of force or power, and of life. I know, from personal experience, I am profoundly conscious that an act of my will is not the same thing as an act of my intellect; that a process of reasoning is not an intuition of truth; and that to love and to syllogize differ one from another. All this I know so well, am so intimately conscious of that I should look on him as excessively unreasonable who would think to prove it to me. Moreover, I am intimately persuaded that my faculties, if exercised aright, tell me the truth; and that to deny this would be to cut from under me the very ground on which I stand. For instance, I am obliged to take my irresistible conviction for granted that I am to-day the same person I was yesterday; that I have not changed my identity. I am conscious, moreover, that, whilst my identity, my self, has remained one and the same, it has passed through many external changes, and has been the subject of endless internal affections and passions; and the testimony of my consciousness as to this fact is primary, and must be taken for granted. I not only am myself now, but have been so from the first; and I am as intimately persuaded that I shall remain so, and shall never be anybody else.

Having thus started with taking for granted my own existence, the identity of self from the first up to now; having taken for granted that my faculties, if properly used, tell me the truth, and not a lie, I proceed a step further, and ask myself whether or not there are asseverations of my faculties, which are so forcible and so luminous in themselves that I am, unless I deny the evidence of those faculties, obliged to admit them as absolute truths? Are there not certain first truths or principles which shine with their own intrinsic light? and does not my whole soul declare to me, not only that they are true as I see them, but true in themselves; and that they would continue true if earth and man were annihilated? And do I not feel, am I not intimately conscious, that to deny such truths an objective value or existence would be to throw all science and reasoning to the winds? I am conscious of my own existence; I cannot prove it. I firmly believe that my faculties, when duly exercised, do not deceive me; I cannot prove this. I have a supreme conviction that to lie, to kill and to blaspheme are in themselves crimes, and never could be made virtues; and that there is a moral law, as well as an intellectual one; and that my fellow-man exists, and that a world is spread out before my feet, which is full of evidences of order and design, and of more than human resources in its extreme variety and beauty.

Such are some of the truths which the intellect must be furnished with before it sets out on its quest after truth. I think every "man of good will" and average ability will see and admit that, in taking these truths as a *locus standi*, I am not taking up too much ground, or asking them to admit anything that does not, on the face of it, demand imperatively the assent of reasonable men. If there should be any who think it worth their while to deny these truths, I, for my part, do not think it worth my while to argue with them.

Having thus prepared the ground on which to erect my structure of Christianity, having thus laid down the principles common to Christians and reasonable men, I now proceed, in conclusion, to show the bearing and tendency of science in the direction of religion, to indicate the remarkable fact that, though science does not, and, from its nature, cannot, prove religion true, still at every turn it gives hints and indications and warnings, which point, one and all, indirectly, and at a distance, it may be, like the deep-down rumblings of some volcanic fire-mountain, towards a Power or Being that lives and moves unseen, yet ever present, to the universe of which we form a part. We could not expect Nature or science to do much more than this: as coming from Him who made all things, and impresses His law and hand on all, it could not do much less. Had it been otherwise, were there no Divine Personal Creator and Ruler, then, at once, no doubt endless, most startling contradictions would present themselves at every turn between the testimony given by "Nature" and that which would in such a case be the mere invention and lie of man. The very fact of the existence of an indirect testimony from science to religion, considering the innumerable and bold teachings of religion, is in itself a startling corroboration in favor of its

Divine origin and of its truth. Would it have been possible, were it a mere creation of the mind of man, without any basis in the order of truth, for it to have kept so clear of the verified discoveries of science, and would it not, long ere this, have continually flatly contradicted them, and lost itself without possibility of redemption? After advanced thinkers, who are antagonistic to religion, have exerted all their talent in bringing their most formidable artillery to bear upon the strongholds of religion, Nature herself turns round upon them, and spontaneously offers more striking signs favorable to the Christian thesis than they are enabled to offer in its disparagement. They cannot touch "Nature," so saturated is it with something above and beyond mere dead matter, without eliciting from it voices in our favor, which they would fain stifle, or make to preach another Gospel than that which we so deeply prize, and which they, by some fatal twist in their moral natures, have so profound an aversion for.

To give as an example out of many more instances in which science seems to favor, or at least to tend towards, the teachings of religion, I will read to you the very words themselves of four of our foremost scientific men with regard to that hidden power which seems to support the world in which we live. Whilst these able writers declare that there is a something, a power behind the veil as it were of material things, they frankly declare that, from the standpoint of their science, they are unable to grapple with it.

Professor Stokes, in his presidential address to the British Association at Exeter, said:

"Admitting to the full as highly probable, though not completely demonstrated, the applicability to living beings of the laws which have been ascertained with reference to dead matter, I feel constrained at the samd time to admit the existence of a mysterious *something* lying beyond, a something *sui generis*, which I regard, not as balancing and suspending the ordinary physical laws, but as working with them and through them to the attainment of a designed end. What this *something* which we call life may be is a profound mystery. . . . When from the phenomena of life we pass on to those of mind, we enter a region still more profoundly mysterious. We can readily imagine that we may here be dealing with phenomena altogether transcending those of mere life, in some such way as those of life transcend, as I have endeavored to infer, those of chemistry and molecular attractions, or as the laws of chemical affinity in their turn transcend those of mere mechanics. Science can be expected to do but little to aid us here, since the instrument of research is itself the object of investigation. It can but enlighten us as to the depth of our ignorance, and lead us to look to a higher aid for that which most nearly concerns our well-being."

Then the famous Dr. Thomas Young says, in his lectures on "Natural Philosophy," touching on an unseen world: "Besides this porosity, there is still room for the supposition that even the ultimate particles of matter may be permeable to the causes of attractions of various kinds, especially if those causes be immaterial; nor is there anything in the unprejudiced study of physical philosophy that that can induce us to doubt the existence of immaterial substances; on the contrary, we see analogies that lead us almost directly to such an opinion. The electrical fluid is supposed to be essentially different from common matter; the general medium of light and heat, according to some, or the principle of coloric, according to others, is equally distinct from it. We see forms of matter, differing in subtlety and nobility, under the names of solids, liquids and gases; above these are the semi-material existences, which produce the phenomena of electricity and magnetism, and either coloric or a universal ether. Higher still, perhaps, are causes of gravitation, and the immediate agents in attractions of all kinds, which exhibit some phenomena apparently still more remote from all that is compatible with material bodies. And of these diffcrent orders of beings, the more refined and immaterial appears to pervade freely the grosser. It seems, therefore, natural to believe that the analogy may be continued still further, until it rises into existences absolutely immaterial and spiritual. We know not but that thousands of spiritual worlds may exist unseen forever by human eyes; nor have we any reason to suppose that even the presence of matter, in a given spot, necessarily excludes these existences from it. Those who maintain that nature always teems with life, wherever living beings can be placed, may therefore speculate with freedom on the possibility of independent worlds; some existing in different parts of space, others pervading each other unseen and unknown, in the same space, and others again to which space may not be a necessary mode of existence."

Even Mr. Herbert Spencer, who is the foremost thinker of the Negative school in England, is forced to admit the existence of a Power behind phenomena, which is beyond his reach. He says, in his "First Principles:" "We are obliged to regard every phenomenon as a manifestation of some Power by which we are acted upon; though omnipotence is unthinkable, yet, as experience discloses no bounds to the diffusion of phenomena, we are unable to think of limits to the presence of this Power, while the criticisms of science teach us that this Power is incomprehensible."

Professor Jevons carries us a step further, and actually solves a difficulty which is a stumbling-block to many minds:

"The hypothesis," says Professor Jevons, "that there is a Creator, at once all-powerful and all-benevolent, is surrounded, as it must seem to every candid investigator, with difficulties verging closely on logical contradiction. The existence of the smallest amount of pain and evil would seem to show that he is either not perfectly benevolent, or not all-powerful. No one can have lived long without experiencing sorrowful events of which the significance is inexplicable. But if we cannot succeed in avoiding contradiction in our notions of elementary geometry, can we expect that the ultimate purposes of existence shall present themselves to us with perfect clearness? I can see nothing to forbid the notion that in a higher state of intelligence much that is now obscure may become clear. We perpetually find ourselves in the position of finite minds attempting infinite problems, and can we be sure that where we see contradiction an infinite intelligence might not discover perfect logical harmony?" ("Pinciples of Science," vol. ii, p. 468.)

Now, there is a saying that a straw will show which way the wind blows, and I do not think I shall be accused of exaggeration in saying that the impression left upon a reasonably cautious mind after carefully reading those extracts in the light of Christian teaching is to the effect that when "Nature" is interrogated regarding some of Religion's fundamental propositions, though it is not able to speak clearly, still it gives signs and hints of agreement with those propositions, and, as far as it goes, seems to tell us that underneath that thin rind which science can pierce, underneath that gross matter with which alone it is able to deal, there is a something, a power, which it is bound to admit, but which it is unable to analyze or explain, and which was Religion's boast before Science, which is essentially of modern times, commenced its operations, or was dreamt of.

Nor is this silent evidence confined to the testimonies of natural science. To show how Religion seems to held her own unscathed in the midst of so many and such formidable, such violent opponents. I will detain you one moment longer, whilst I show how even the Bible itself, which existed and was believed in centuries before modern criticism come to light, holds its own in the face of the deepest, most indefatigable and most ingenious research. Cardinal Wiseman, in his " Connection between Science and Revealed Religion" (p. 353), thus sums up the result of scientific investigation in its bearing on the Sacred text:

"Not indeed," he says, "that there has been any lack of abundant differences of reading; on the contrary, the number is overpowering. Mill's first effort produced thirty thousand, and the number may be said to daily increase. But in all this mass, although every attainable source has been exhausted, although the Fathers of every age have been gleaned for their readings, although the versions of every nation, Arabic, Syriac, Coptic, Armenian and Ethiopian, have been ransacked for their renderings, although manuscripts of every age, from the sixteenth upwards to the third, and of every country, have been again and again visited by industrious swarms to rifle them of their treasures; although, having exhausted all the stores of the West, critics have travelled, like naturalists, into distant lands to discover new specimens, have visited, like Scholz or Sebastiana, the recesses of Mount Athos, or the unexplored libraries of the Egyptian and Syrian deserts, yet nothing has been discovered, no, not one single various reading which can throw doubt upon any passage before considered certain or decisive, in favor of any important doctrine."

I believe it will be found that the more religion and science are studied scientifically, so much the more will they confirm each other's true positions, and that the more those apparent propositions are probed and tested that are trumpeted forth by men who are rather the athletes of Atheism than the calm investigators of Nature, so much the more surely will they assume their proper shape, and offer no resistance to religious truth. Did scientific men avoid the three errors in method pointed out by Bacon in his "Advancement of Learning" (pp. 33, 34, 94, 95, Markby's Ed.), they would not make so many mistakes.

1. In dealing with the merits of their own particular science, they are too apt to stand on the dead level of that science. Whereas Bacon tells them that "no perfect discovery can be made upon a flat or a level; neither is it possible to discover the more remote and deeper parts of any science if you stand upon the level of the same science, and ascend not to a higher science."

2. Secondly, they, like other men, and perhaps somewhat more than most men, are apt to think and to act upon the thought that their particular science is able to do a great deal more than it can do, and are in frequent danger of riding their intellectual hobbies to death. "Another error," continues Bacon, "which hath some connection with this latter is, that men have used to infect their meditations, opinions and doctrines with some conceits which they have most admired, or some sciences which they have most applied."

3. Thirdly, they are continually confusing the physical and moral orders, and delight in the idea of being able to

point out some repugnance between them. Bacon says this confusion is an error. "Not because," says he, "those final causes are true and worthy to be inquired, being kept within their own province, but because their excursions into the limits of physical causes hath bred a vastness and solitude in that track. For otherwise, keeping their precincts and borders, *men are extremely deceived if they think there is an enmity or repugnance at all between them.*"

It is on account of the non-observance of these rules that some scientific men, with like passions with other men, create confusion and scandal in the popular mind, endeavoring not to show the points of reconciliation between the higher and the lower sciences, but rather striving from the dead level of their own especial branch, and sometimes through mere pugnacity, to confound and confuse together things that should be separate, and to bring, by so doing, the traditions of ages and the most venerable dogmata into contempt.

I have, then, now completed my task for this evening. I have introduced you to the subject matter of my Arguments; I have pointed out to you what I am attempting to do; why I dread the task and yet am urged to undertake it. I have defined, as well as I can, my terms; I have indicated my starting-point and the *locus standi*, which is to be common to me and my audience; I have told you to whom, exclusively, I am about to address myself; I have shown how the bearing of Natural Science is in the direction of religion, and that its testimonies, taken in the main and on the whole, offer a remarkable evidence to the oneness of that source from which both Nature and Grace proceed. "No one," says an able writer, "who has paid a serious attention to the progress of the modern sciences, can entertain a doubt that all the really substantiated discoveries which have been supposed to contravene Christianity, do in reality only deepen its profundity and emphasize its indispensable necessity for men. Never before, in all the history of mankind, has the Deity seemed so awful, so remote from man, so mighty in the tremendous forces that He wields, so majestic in the permanence and tranquillity of His resistless will. Never before has man realized his own excessive smallness and imp'tence; his inability to destroy, much more to create, one atom or molecule? his dependence for life, for thought, for character even, on the material environment of which he once thought himself master." And, finally, I have pointed out three principal rocks on which men of science are apt to split; so that we may, in our four Arguments in favor of Christianity, do all that in us lies to avoid them.

Next Sunday evening I purpose to speak of "Man," and to show you how his nature and faculties point towards those truths which are maintained by the Christian School, but which the Negative School denies.

MAN.

On Sunday, March 6, His Grace Archbishop Vaughn delivered his second Lenten discourse at the pro-Cathedral, on the subject "Man." Long before 7 o'clock the available space in the building was packed, and large numbers were unable to gain admittance. There must have been over four thousand people present. There was a large number of clergymen and laymen seated around His Grace in the sanctuary. In the congregation were many Protestant gentlemen. His Grace said :—

Last Sunday night I endeavored in my Introductory Address to clear the ground before us by defining terms, pointing out our *locus standi*, and indicating in a general way the limits of science and the errors into which, in their method, some so-called scientific men are only too ready to fall. I, moreover, adduced some reasons for the opinion that the more "Nature" is properly interrogated, so much the more does she give signs and hints and indistinct indications of the existence of those truths which are taught by the Christian scheme. I took some little pains to bring out the fact that, after all, if Science keeps scientifically to its province, it can tell us comparatively very little regarding that which we care most to know about. As to cataloguing and ticketing shells and fossils, and explaining the habits and functions of animate nature, that has its use and interest; but is not to be compared to the interest which we feel in those higher spheres of knowledge into which Science, from the nature of the case, is not privileged to enter. It is of some importance to remember this; for if it be true that Science is bound down to this comparatively humble sphere of action; if it be true that it has no business to raise its voice in dogmatically declaring what life, and matter, and mind are, and their origin and destiny, and what God is; if it has no vocation to enter the lists in these fundamental positions, so essentially connected with religion; surely, if this be the case, we may be somewhat surprised that scientific men should thus dogmatize, or that any one should imagine that Science and Religion could possibly be in antagonism.

To convince you that the tendency of some leading scientific men to dogmatize and assert, instead of to prove and verify, has a real existence, and is exerting a mischievous influence at the present hour, I need but remind you of the celebrated Virchow's address before the Association of German Naturalists and Physicians at Munich in 1877. Speaking of the doctrine of man having been evolved out of matter or protoplasm, he says: "All this is very fine and admirable, and may ultimately prove true. It is *possible*. . . . I have no objection to your saying that atoms of carbon also possess mind, or that in their connection with the Plastidule-company they acquire mind; only *I do not know how I am to perceive this*. It is a mere playing with words. . . . The processes of the human mind *may* ultimately find a chemical explanation; but at present, in my opinion, it is not my business to bring these provinces into connection. . . . Throughout this discourse I am not asserting that it will never be possible to bring psychical processes into an immediate connection with those which are physical. All I say is, that we have at *present* no right to set up this possible connection as a *doctrine* of science; and I must enter my decided protest against the attempt to make a premature extension of our doctrines in this manner, and to be ever anew thrusting into the very foreground of our expositions that which has so often proved an insoluble problem." He continues: "I am persuaded that only by such resignation, imposed by us on ourselves and practised towards the rest of the world, shall we be able to conduct the contest with our opponents, and to carry it on to victory. Every attempt to transform our problems into doctrines, to introduce our hypotheses as the bases of introduction—especially the attempt simply to dispossess the Church, and to supplant its dogmas forthwith by a religion of evolution—be assured, gentlemen, every such attempt will make shipwreck, and its wreck will also bring with it the greatest perils for the whole position of Science. Therefore, let us moderate our zeal; let us patiently resign ourselves always to put forward, as problems only, even the most favorite problems that we set up; never ceasing to repeat a hundred-fold a hundred times: 'Do not take this for established truth; be prepared to find it otherwise; only for the moment we are of opinion that it may possibly be so.'"

Professor Tyndal, who made himself conspicuous, not to say notorious, as a Materialist, in his celebrated Belfast Address, frankly acknowledges that Science is surrounded by mysteries on all sides, while at the same time he lets out, almost in spite of himself, that irrepressible yearning after another world and a Divine Being which is found at the heart of every seriously intelligent man. "As regards knowledge," he says, "physical science is polar. In one sense it knows, or is destined to know, everything. In another sense it knows nothing. Science understands much of this intermediate phase of things that we call Nature, of which it is the product; but science knows nothing of the origin or destiny of Nature. Who or what made the sun, or gave his rays their alleged power? Who or what made and bestowed upon the ultimate particles of matter their wondrous power of varied interaction? Science does not know; the mystery, though pushed back, remains unaltered. To many of us who feel that there are more things in heaven and earth than are dreamt of in the present philosophy of Science, but who have been taught by baffled efforts how vain is the attempt to grapple with the Inscrutable, the ultimate frame of mind is that of Goethe:

> Who dares to name His Name,
> Or belief in Him proclaim,
> Veiled in mystery as He is, the All-enfolder?
> Gleams across the mind His light,
> Feels the lifted soul His might,
> Dare it then deny His reign the All-upholder?

("Fragments of Science," p. 644-5.) Though I cannot understand how Tyndal or Goethe could feel much difficulty in daring to "proclaim belief in God" if they did not "dare to deny His reign;" though I can scarcely imagine a more grotesque "ultimate frame of mind" or "intellectual position" than that; still it is something for them to be so over-pressed by the arguments of God's existence and governance as to make them hold their tongues, whilst reasonable men are enforcing its truth with every possible variety of argument. Anyhow, this seems to be the position of Science; it cannot deny, and dare not, for it would contradict its own canons if it did; it cannot affirm "a belief," and dare not, for Science has nothing to do with belief, but with experiment and verification, after having taken a number of things for granted. The most we can expect it to do for us is to present us with fresh and fresh evidences of the power and wisdom of that All-wise Being with whose works it is ever coming in contact.

Having thus let Science down gently into its legitimate place, I will now proceed, without delay, to develop the first Argument that comes on my list touching the reasonableness of Christianity and the shallowness of Unbelief. This first Argument is founded on the origin and character and faculties of man. No subject could be imagined of greater interest to all of us than that which has to do with our own species, and with the position which we ourselves hold in this universe of which we form a part. The proper study of man-kind is Man, and with that study we shall be engaged this evening. Indeed, it not only is most interesting personally, and a proper study for all mankind, but, what is more to the purpose, it is a study of the highest scientific importance at the present day. Mr. Mott, in his remarkable address " On the Origin of Savage Life," says most truly, and Mr. Mivart endorses his words, that " questions concerning the origin of mankind have become either the radiating or the culminating points in most branches of science;" and, therefore, in treating of this subject, I am entering straight into the arena with my opponents, and am joining issue on a fundamental question, upon which not merely the past, but the future, of the race depends.

What, then, is the teaching of the Negative School with regard to the race of which we form a portion? What does this school proclaim as the out-come of " Science " regarding the origin of this large and distinguished assemblage which is listening to my words? If a disciple of this school were standing in my place he would tell you that Science had achieved another victory in the discovery of your origin; and he would most probably express himself as follows: " You desire, my dear friends to know what you really are. I am a scientific man, I am a votary of verification and research, and I take nothing for granted, but prove everything as I slowly advance along the arduous path of true enlightenment. I have felt that the proper study of mankind is man, and that most momentous interests depend upon the right interpretation of facts connected with our noble species. You naturally desire to know what you are, or rather whence you come, so that you may make a guess whither you are going. Well, after deep study and untiring scrutiny, I, that is to say, Science, which takes nothing for granted, have come to the distinct conclusion that you have been evolved into your actual state of comparative perfection from the dirt beneath your feet. To have arrived at your present position you have gone through innumerable changes for the better. Just before you became men you were monkeys, before monkeys mudfish. Of all existing apes, my great master, Mr. Darwin, says that you are immediately descended from the broad-breast-boned group; and that the gorilla, of all the animal creation, is most like you in appearance. True, you have the wrist-bones of the chimpanzee, the legs of a gibbon, the bridging convolutions of the long-tailed thumbless spider monkey, and the voice of the long-armed ape; and, therefore, we are more inclined on the whole to believe that you are somehow or other related, in this way or that, with all the various species of monkeys that can be found in the old and new worlds. Whatever be the case, you began your being from the lowest and most brutal stage of existence; and by a marvellous process of bettering yourselves you have at last arrived at your present happy condition. But mark you, this is the great and never-to-be-forgotten discovery of science, namely, that, though it admits that you have out-stripped all your fellow-monkeys in the race of life, still it has found out, and you must ever firmly bear it in mind, that the difference between you and the lowest brute in the field is merely a difference of degree, not a difference of kind. You all belong to the same happy family; and some amongst you have bettered yourselves, and others have not. Hence, you see you started with a very poor stock-in-trade for getting on in the world. Your distant ancestors were dumb as brutes are dumb; they could speak no articulate tongue; they had no idea of moral duty, of right or wrong, no freedom of will, no soul, they were veritable brute beasts, without reason and without conscience, without notion of virtue or of honor, and, in point of fact, could in no way be distinguished from those irrational beasts which are now served up to you for food. This is, I know, not very flattering; but science is science, and it is our duty to hail its victories with joy, whatever the consequences may be. You may pride yourselves on calling yourselves ladies and gentlemen, but to speak scientifically, a Newton, a Shakespeare, a Dante, or St. Augustine, does not differ in kind, but only in degree, from the gorilla, the chimpanzee or the baboon; and if such men as these are so situated, you might bear with patient resignation the destruction of your ancient superstitions." Or to speak seriously, in the words of Elam, "As Virchow observes, it is not altogether the question what we ourselves mean by our theories, expressed with 'modest reserve,' as what the rough and trenchant logic of the outer world makes of it. And *this* is what is made of the Evolution doctrine generally: The dog has just as long a pedigree as we have; he descends from the same original pair of vertebrata; and, tracing these backwards, our common origin was a molecule or protoplasm, which had been formed, by mechanical force, from carbon, hydrogen, oxygen and nitrogen. What essential difference, then, is there between man and the dog, and why should we hesitate to do to the one what we do daily to the other?"*

All this sounds very grotesque, very absurd, and very empty talk. But, for all that, I have not exaggerated the position of the Negative School in their account of the origin of man. They declare that "Science" has made this discovery, and, overawed by the dogmatic and bold assertion of those who, by means of the word "Science," impose upon the multitude, thousands are beginning to believe that, after all, they are merely animals, with sharper faculties than others, who have to live their day upon the earth, and then to die into it again. I need not ask you to figure to yourselves the chaos society would be thrown into if such a doctrine as this became wildly acted upon and popular. Now, my object to-night is to show that this doctrine of the Negative School is shallow, and that man is different, not merely in degree, but in kind, from the brute creation ; that man is not a bestial animal, which, by a process of gradual improvement, has at last grown out of being a bestial animal into being a man, but that he is separated by an impassable gulf from the brute creation, and possesses endowments and attributes which, in the eyes of any reasonable person, would place him as a man at once in a category by himself, far out of the reach of the highest form of mere irrational animal existences. Now, the theory of the Negative School is, that man has arrived from the brutal stage to his present perfection by going through a long, almost or quite imperceptible course of evolutions in the direction of improvement, throwing off the brute by slow processes and degrees, and putting on the man. If such be really the case, surely we ought to be able to light upon specimens in their various stages of transition, just as

---

*Not an imaginary address.

we may see on some trees, buds, flowers and fruits developing at one time towards their perfection. But do we see this? Have these scientific men ever seen it? Has any traveller ever imagined that he has seen anything of the kind? If the transition be so very gradual, how does it happen that there are not thousands on thousands of creatures approaching so near to being men, and yet keeping so near to being animals, that no one can tell which they are? As a practical matter of fact, have you ever read of any travellers or explorers coming upon a race of creatures in any part of the globe, however savage and unknown, which puzzled them for one single instant as to whether they were men or brutes? Have any of these bold adventurers ever by mistake shot a man, thinking him to be a brute, and sent his skin as a curiosity, or a new discovery, to his friends at home, or to some scientific society? It may be difficult to draw the line between the exact beginning of day and the ending of night, but I have never heard of any difficulty in knowing a man when you see him from an irrational brute. And why? Because they are separated by a radical difference, by a dividing line which forever separates man from those animals over which he exerts so sovereign a mastery.

Allow me to bring before your attention a living argument in favor of the truth of what I say. If it could be proved that the most degraded type of man, the lowest form known, possessed qualities and characteristics which are common to him with all civilized men, and which animals do not possess, if it could be shown that he was thus cut off from the brute creation by profound radical differences, surely it would reasonably follow that he would also differ in his origin from irrational nature; being radically different and *sui generis* in faculties and powers, he would reasonably be conceived as different, not merely in degree, but in *kind*, from the brute creation. Now, which is generally looked upon as the lowest type that has yet been discovered? According to Mr. Mivart, a very high authority, and I believe his view is generally adopted by those who have had much experience of savage life in various parts of the globe, the aborigines of Australia exhibit the lowest form of humanity that has yet been found. They, it is said, are nearest to the brute creation. "As we have said," says Mr. Mivart, "the native Australians have much pretension to the post of lowest of existing races." In another place he remarks: "The Australians are generally believed to be the most hopeless subjects of missionary effort." And of all Australian tribes, the most savage and inhuman are those who dwell in the north, about the Gulf of Carpentaria. Such, then, being the case, I ask, would it not be a fair test to secure one of these lowest specimens, and examine whether or no he possess, at least in rudiment, those faculties and characteristics which are common to all men, and which no brute has ever been known even to simulate? If it were, at first sight, or after a short experiment, evident that one of these savages, or one of their children, which would be better, possessed the same mental endowments, the same in kind, if not in degree, as any ordinary Christian; would it not be reasonable to conclude that they belonged to the same family, and that that family was separated by a gulf which was impassable from the animals of the field, or the various varieties of apes?

Fortunately, I am in a position to prove to you, by a practical demonstration, that this lowest race amongst mankind does possess such qualities as all men are endowed with, and which all irrational animals lack. I have but to give you the history of "Bobby," the little black boy, who accompanied me this evening, dressed in cassock and surplice, into your presence. This little black boy, who is now going through his studies with the Marist Brothers of St. Patrick's, represents the living argument to which I refer. When I first arrived in this colony, it happened that a man came to the Vicar-General's office, and asked if he could see me. I had an interview with him. He told me he was going home, having been very successful in digging for gold in the North of Queensland. But there was one difficulty in the way. He had brought down a little black child from the Gulf of Carpentaria, whose parents had died, or had been killed. He had brought the child to Sydney; and, as he thought it would probably die of cold if taken to England, he was anxious to find some one who would be willing to take the child and keep it, and be kind to it. And, having heard my name, he made so bold, he said, to ask me to do this act of charity. I consented on the condition that I should see the boy first, so as to make sure that he was not a white boy with a black face. I think the child must then have been about five or six years old. Here he is before you. Now this child had been brought straight down from the Gulf of Carpentaria· He came fresh and clean from his native forest; and would bring with him in his person the genuine and unadulterated characteristics of that savage tribe to which he was said to belong. Here, then, was a living example, exhibiting itself in all its native reality, of the lowest and most savage type of humanity that is extant on the earth. And not only a living example, but one in the first years of existence, with merely the germs of its powers in any exercise; and almost rudimentary in its development of body and mind.

Now, what did I find in this young specimen of an Aboriginal Australian? Did I find the smallest possible difficulty in knowing him to be a human being? Did I imagine it possible for a moment that he was of the mere brute creation? Far from it. He was human and rational and intelligent, and as much the child of human parents as any child that has ever been born. Though he could only speak a word or two of English, he could speak the language of his tribe; he had a sense of duty, and knew the difference between duty and pleasure; he knew the difference between wright and wrong, between justice of which he had a very keen sense, and injustice; and seemed penetrated with religious ideas, especially with regard to a Divine Being, and future reward and punishment. That at his age he could have learnt these things before I saw him from the whites, or that he had been taught them by my friend, who gave him over to my custody, I do not think possible; but I firmly believe this, that he possessed the traditions of his race, which, when added to the spontaneous dictates of his natural faculties and conscience, is sufficient to account for his possessing—belonging, as he did, to the lowest race of all—those especial characteristics which are found more or less in all mankind, but which are never to be found in any, not even in the highest types of irrational creatures. Had the Brothers any difficulty in receiving "Bobby" into their school? Did it ever enter the heads of his companions to mistake him for anything but what he was—a little black boy—in more ways than one more intelligent and smart than the best amongst them? And has he not shown, in his progress in his lessons, that he has all the faculties and gifts which civilized men possess? And, on the other hand, who has ever sent to school a creature which puzzled people as to whether it was a brute beast or a rational being? Has any one heard or read of such a doubt ever being entertained? And, if no one has, how is it that, with such an everlasting gulf between all men on the one side, and all animals on the other, that "foremost thinkers" and "scientific" men should try and persuade the public that man is evolved from a mud-fish, and was once an animal so near an ape, and yet not one, that no one could tell what he was, and then became a full-grown ape; and then, by going through untold processes, became so near a man, and yet not a man, that no one could tell whether he was a man or not; till, after a course of other evolutionary processes, he became so much a man that the whole world declared, except Mr. Darwin, and some others who follow him, that he could never have been an ape at all, and must always have been a man. How is it that we cannot put a finger on one single specimen of a man so near an ape as to be a confusion to us; or an ape so near a man as to feel inclined to invite him to dinner, and give him the benefit of the doubt? Let men of science prove and verify their theories before they deliver them to the world as facts; and let the world remember that "Science" is only a name, like "Theology;" and that everything that goes by the name of Science is not Science; some of the things going by that name being merely the crude suppositions of eratic minds who wish to be talked about, or to create a sensation, or to cast stones at the teachings of the Gospel. My own practical experience in regard to little "Bobby" is borne out by the following words of Mr. Mivart with regard to the religious notion of the aborigines: "As we have said, the native Australians have much pretension to the post of lowest of existing races, and we often hear a great deal as to their non-religious condition; nevertheless, Mr. Tylor quotes the Rev. W. Ridley to the effect that, 'whenever he has conversed with the aborigines, he found them to have quite definite traditions concerning supernatural beings, as Baime, whose voice they hear in thunder, and who made all things.' Moreover, this testimony is reinforced by that of Stanbridge (T. Eth. Soc. vol. i., p. 301), who is quoted as asserting that, so far from the Australians having no religion, 'they declare that Jupiter, whom they call "foot of day" (Ginabong-Beary), was a chief among the old Spirits, that ancient race who were translated to heaven before man came on earth.'" ("Lessons from Nature," p. 140.)

The account given by Monsignor Salvado of the aborigines of Western Australia points in the same direction. He tells us, says Max Muller, that they believe in an Omnipotent Being, creator of heaven and earth, whom they call *Motogon*, and whom they imagine as a very tall, powerful and wise man of their own country and complexion. His mode of creation was by breathing; to create the earth he said, "Earth come forth!" and he breathed, and the earth was created. So with the sun, the tree and the kangaroo, etc. *Motogon*, the author of life, is confronted with Cienga, the author of death. This latter being is the unchainer of the whirlwind and the storm, and the invisible author of the death of their children, wherefore the natives fear him exceedingly.

Thus, from personal knowledge of one of the lowest of our race, and from the testimony of independent authorities, I come to the conclusion that the more we probe this question, so much the more shall we have reason to be convinced that man, even in the lowest of his species, is different absolutely in kind from the brute creation. Indeed, that wave of scientific discovery which threatened, some few years back, to carry all before it is sinking beneath the level, and a reaction is setting in towards the Christian view, which men of science could not baffle, and are beginning, if not to adopt, to treat with less of their unscientific contempt. Eighteen years' study have not, in this question, advanced Mr. Huxley's view one iota. Indeed, cautious scientific men are gradually retiring from an untenable position; whilst the results of their laborious and sleepless investigations have been, taking them as a whole, ever so many arguments or weapons which the philosopher can seize to great advantage, and turn towards the defence, in an indirect manner, of religious truth. In order to give a vigorous shake to the foundation of this supposed scientific discovery, viz: that men are brutes, I will simply read you the words of unexceptionable witnesses, men of high renown in their respective countries—I mean Professor Huxley, and Virchow, the great philosopher. Huxley says, regarding man's having been once an ape: "I must confess that my opinion remains exactly where it was some eighteen years ago. . . I did then put forward the opinion that what is known as the Neanderthal skull is, of human remains, that which presents the most marked and definite characteristics of a lower type, using the language in the same sense as we would use it in other branches of zoology. I believe it to belong to the lowest form of human being of which we have any knowledge, and we know, from the remains accompanying that human being, that, as far as all fundamental points of structure were concerned, he was as much a man —could wear boots just as easily—as any of us; so that I think the question remains much where it was, I don't know that there is any reason for doubting that the men who existed at that day were, in all essential respects, similar to the men who exist now." Mr. Huxley made this important declaration only the other day, at the meeting of the British Association. Now, observe this for a moment. Here we have, on the one hand, a living specimen of the lowest type of the human race, possessing all the gifts and faculties of an ordinary man; and here we have, on the other, the skull and remains of the lowest type, supposed to have lived ages ago, and possessing, according to the unimpeachable authority of Mr. Huxley, all the essentials of mankind. How is it that both these lowest types, the living boy and the dead skeleton, point so straight in the same direction, so unmistakably towards the rational creature; whilst they, as it were, turn their backs as much as we do on the brute creation? To this there seems to be but one rational reply: Because men are ever men, and brutes always brutes.

So far for Mr. Huxley. What now does Virchow say? "One thing I must say," says he, addressing the *savants* at Munich, "that not a single fossil skull of an ape or of an 'ape-man' has yet been found that could really have belonged to a human being. Every addition to the amount of objects which we have obtained as materials for discussion has removed us further from the hypothesis propounded. . . As a matter of fact, we must positively recognize that there still exists as yet a sharp line of demarcation between man and the ape. *We cannot teach, we cannot pronounce it to be a conquest of Science, that man descends from the ape or from any other animal.* We can only indicate it as an hypothesis, however probable it may seem, and however obvious a solution it may appear." ("The Freedom of Science in the Modern State," p. 62-3. The marks of emphasis are from the original.)

Having now given a fair shake to the foundations of the supposed scientific discovery, that men are brutes, I now proceed to upset those foundations a little more, that is to say, to show all reasonable men that the whole bearing of the evidence upon this momentous question is in the direction of the Christian creed; and that the more studiously the lowest type of men is compared with the highest type of brutes, so much the more firmly is there reason to be persuaded that man was never a brute, and a brute has never been developed into a man; that the two categories are divided, in one word, by so clear and rigid a line, that any ordinary man can put his finger on it in a moment.

I start, then, with asking the question, Is it absolutely certain that mankind has been in a state of steady progression from the protoplasm to his present state? Is it absolutely demonstrated, as it should be before it is treated as an established fact, that the low-class savage grew steadily up to his present position through infinite evolutionary processes, and that, so far as he goes, he is now simply more advanced than ever he was before, and is going on advancing towards higher developments and perfections? Is it impossible that the savage may be rather a degenerate man than an elevated animal? If we could push back through his previous history, should we not find, at least in large instances, that his ancestors, instead of being apes and baboons, were far more highly civilized than he, and that, through isolation and other causes, he lost those high qualities which distinguish those from whom he sprang? If such be the case, at the very start our opponents' ape theory is thrown into inextricable confusion. If it cannot be shown in any one single instance that man has evolved himself from irrational bruteism, and if, on the other hand, it can be shown that, in large instances, he has simply degenerated from a higher culture and civilization, why may we not rationally suppose that such has been the case with others, though we have not the means of making the discovery? "We may be certain," says Mivart, "that some savages have been degraded from a higher level, and this certainly establishes an *a priori* probability that all have been so." ("Lessons from Nature," p. 154).

Speaking of savages, Mr. Herbert Spencer says: "Probably most of them, *if not all of them*, had ancestors in higher states; and among their beliefs remain some which were evolved during those higher states. While the degradation theory, so currently held, is untenable, the theory of progression, taken in its unqualified form, seems to me untenable also. If, on the one hand, the notion that savagery is caused by lapse from civilization is irreconcilable with evidence, there is, on the other hand, inadequate warrant for the notion that the lowest savagery has always been as low as it is now. It is quite possible, and, I believe, highly probable, that retrogression has been as frequent as progression. . . . That supplanting of race by race, and thrusting into corners such inferior races as are not exterminated, which is now going on so actively, and which has been going on from the earliest recorded times, must have been ever going on. And the implication is, that remnants of inferior races, taking refuge in inclement, barren or otherwise unfit regions, have retrograded." ("Principles of Sociology," vol. i, p. 106.)

And we do possess most startling evidences, on a very large scale, of ancient cultures and civilizations, which once flourished, and of which there only remain the unmistakable traces. Take two examples, one of an isolated island and another of a vast continent. Easter Island stands by itself in the Pacific Ocean, two thousand miles from South America, and one thousand from the nearest inhabited island. Mott says that the inhabitants of that island live in the midst of the remains, in the shape of terraces and images, of a former higher civilization, of which they can give no account. He says: "Similar terraces and images have been seen in other islands now uninhabited. The ruins of ancient stone buildings of great extent are found in the Philippine Islands, the Ladrones, the Marshall and Gilbert, the Society Islands, the Navigators, and the Marquesas. They thus extend over ten thousand miles of ocean."

Now, allow me for one moment to transport you in imagination to the Salisbury Museum, in England. Amongst other curiosities, I can imagine the attention of many gentlemen, being attracted to some very artistic-looking tobacco-pipes. Take one of them in your hand. You perceive that they are made of stone, sculptured. Look at the artistic work, done, evidently, by a skillful lapidary. Those birds and animals and human heads that ornament the well-hollowed bowl speak of a civilization, a taste, a leisure, not to be found amongst savage tribes. Look at the tubes through which the smoke was drawn; they have, you will perceive, been drilled with perfect skill. Now, that tobacco-pipe in your hand is the oldest tobacco-pipe in the world. Who made these pipes? They may be said to represent an ancient civilization, long forgotten, which extended, and still gives evidences most unmistakable of its past glories, over the whole of North America, from the Gulf of Mexico to Canada. That civilization is gone. The children of it have degenerated and have lost and forgotten the skill and culture of their fathers; they have not been gradually growing up, but sinking down, in the scale of culture until they have reached the position of simple savages. "These savages," says Mott, "have reached their present state by degradation, and not by progress. Their rude arts are not their own invention, but are derived from higher art, become barbarous in their hands. No single custom found amongst them can be identified as of savage origin, for their former customs were of course those of their more civilized ancestors, and it is these, as altered by barbarism, that we find among them now. But," he continues, "if this is the case over an entire continent, what becomes of the idea that savage life in general is an example of arrested progress, and not an example of retrogression?" (See Mivart's "Lessons," p. 151.)

Frederick Schlegel, whose philosophy of history contains many able generalizations, has long ago suggested a cause which, most assuredly, from what we know ourselves, is enough to account for any depth of degradation, without starting the untenable theory of the protoplasm and the ape. The fall of Adam and the theory of original sin are in complete harmony with the phenomena of human retrogression, that meets our eyes upon so many sides. "When man," says Frederick Schlegel, "had once fallen from virtue, no determinable limit could be assigned to his degradation, nor how far he might descend by degrees, and approximate even to the level of the brute; but, as from his origin he was a being essentially free, he was, in consequence capable of change, and even in his organic powers most flexible. We must adopt this principle, as the only clue to guide us in our inquiries, from the negro, who, as well from his bodily strength and agility, as from his docile, and, in general, excellent character, is far from occupying the lowest grade in the scale of humanity, down to the monstrous Patagonian, the almost imbecile Peshwarais, and the horrible cannibal of New Zealand, whose very portrait excites a shudder in the beholder. So far from seeking, with Rosseau and his disciples, for the true origin of mankind, and the proper foundations of the social compact, in the condition even of the best and noblest savages, we regard it, on the contrary, as a state of degeneracy and degredation." ("Philosophy of History," trans. by Robertson, vol. i, pp. 48, 49.)

Having now brought before your notice the important fact that it has been practically proved that man, on a large scale, has fallen from civilization to barbarism, from a higher estate to a lower; having shown you that even "advanced thinkers" are fighting shy of the Ape theory of our origin; having given you a practical and living example of the lowest races being in every sense a human rational being; having confirmed this fact by what Huxley tells us of the Neanderthal remains and their witness to the same effect; having thus far advanced in the direction of the Christian teaching; having so far proved to you that those who wished to destroy the temple of Religion have merely fortified it in a manner which they least expected; having now got some firm and solid standing-ground, I will proceed to show you that the faculties and mental endowments of the lowest savages testify to the fact that they differ not merely in degree, but absolutely in kind, from the irrational brute creation.

Of course we feel no hesitation in admitting, indeed, we teach and firmly assert, that man, though rational, is also to all intents and purposes, so far as his mere body is concerned, an animal; and being an animal, he is to a greater or less degree, and must be, from the nature of the case, like, whilst in many things unlike, all other animals. We are not entering the lists with our adversaries regarding the animal man, our contention is that his difference in nature springs from another source. "With a certain difference of structure," says Elam, "between the lower apes and gorilla, we find, perhaps, a corresponding, moderate, but certainly *finite* and easily measurable difference of *nature* between them; whilst with a *less marked difference* of structure between the gorilla and man, we have a divergence of nature not to be measured, but 'practically infinite.' Can any more complete or cogent demonstration be desired to show that the specific characteristics of man are not to be defined in terms, or by detail, of his bodily structure? It is by his moral nature, by his capacity for a religious sentiment, by his power of conceiving abstract ideas of truth, justice, right and wrong, by the possession of articulate speech, and of *conscious* reasoning, reflective and volitional faculty, that it is demonstrated that man is neither of nor from the brute; 'that he differs fundamentally from every other creature which presents itself to our senses; that he differs absolutely, and, therefore, differs in origin also.'"

To bring this fact out clearly, I must solicit your patience whilst I read you a passage from one of Dr. Newman's works, which will light up my argument with considerable vividness: The great Oratorian is bringing forward a well-known fable to illustrate his subject, and I am taking the liberty of making use of it to throw a light on mine. "The Man once invited the Lion to be his guest, and received him with princely hospitality. The Lion had the run of a magnificent palace, in which there were a vast many things to admire. There were large saloons and long corridors, richly furnished and decorated, and filled with a profusion of fine specimens of sculpture and painting, the works of the first masters in either art. The subjects represented were various; but the most prominent of them had an especial interest for the noble animal who stalked by them. It was that of the Lion himself; and as the owner of the mansion led him from one apartment to the other, he did not fail to direct his attention to the indirect homage which these various groups and tableaux paid to the importance of the Lion tribe.

"There was, however, one remarkable feature in all of them, to which the host, silent as he was from politeness, seemed not at all insensible; that diverse as were these representations, in one point they all agreed—that the man was always victorious, and the lion was always overcome. The man had it all his own way, and the lion was but a fool, and served to make him sport. There were exquisite works in marble, of Samson rending the lion like a kid, and young David taking the lion by the beard and choking him. There was the man who ran his arm down the lion's throat and held him fast by the tongue; and there was that other who, when carried off in his teeth, contrived to pull a penknife from his pocket and lodge it in the monster's heart. Then there was a lion hunt, or what had been such, for the brute was rolling around in the agonies of death, and his conqueror on his bleeding horse was surveying him from a distance. There was a gladiator from the Roman amphitheatre in mortal struggle with his tawny foe, and it was plain who was getting the mastery. There was a lion in a net, a lion in a trap, four lions yoked in harness were drawing the car of a Roman emperor, and elsewhere stood Hercules, clad in the lion's skin, and with the club that demolished him.

"Nor was this all. The lion was not only triumphed over, mocked, spurned, but he was tortured into extravagant forms, as if he were not only the slave and creature, but the very creation of man. He became an artistic decoration, and an heraldic emblazonment. The feet of alabaster tables fell away into lions' paws; lions' faces grinned on each side the shining mantelpiece, and lions' mouths held tight the handles of the doors. There were sphynxes, too, half lion, half woman; there were lions rampant holding flags, lions couchant, lions passant, lions regardant, lions and unicorns; there were lions white, black and red; in short, there was no misconception or excess of indignity which was thought too great for the lord of the forest and the king of brutes. After he had gone over the mansion, his entertainer asked him what he thought of the splendors it contained, and he in reply did full justice to the riches of its owner and the skill of its decorators; but, he added, 'lions would have fared better had lions been the artists.'" ("Lectures on Catholicism in England," pp. 2, 4.)

The appositeness and liveliness of this extract must be my excuse for its length. Now, how does it bear on my subject? In this way: it brings out two things most vividly. First, the fact that man's intellectual and mental faculties, his soul, that which is best and highest in him, separates him absolutely and at once from the highest brute animal that ever was. The lion's enormous physical strength merely reflects and throws out into bold relief the vast superiority of intellect as compared with it; secondly, the very grotesqueness of the idea of a lion being capable of accompanying a man through his house, and behaving like a reasonable being, shows at once that the lion and the man have nought in common except the fact of both possessing animal frames and organs. Why have not lions been artists? Because they never possessed those faculties which are required for exercising art. The whole picture of the fable, so far as man's position is concerned, is not strained in the least; there is not an action or a position described, which has not or may not have easily been actually realized; and the picture of man's dominion over the kings of the brute creation, as thus described, is not exaggerated or overdrawn. How is it that there is this vast gulf between the lion and the man—between the man and the brute? It is because man possesses a soul and mental endowments; has an intellect, a reasoning faculty, a free will, of which he is conscious, a knowledge of good and evil, a moral sense, and a religious sentiment and aspiration. It is because man has self-consciousness as well as a conscience; because he knows himself to be a responsible being: and thus, possessing an intellectual nature of this description, notwithstanding the overwhelming physical power of the lion, man is his undoubted lord and master, and will remain so to the end. Man will ever be painting the lion; the lion will never paint the man; the man will never be able to do one thing which the fable says he did—to take the lion round his house, and converse and reason with him; for the lion will never be able to speak, never to reason, or intellectually understand, never able to restrain his nature, through a sense of politeness or any other sense, or to conceive the idea of what an artist is, much less to suggest that a lion should become one.

Take now the lowest savage and compare him with the king of beasts. Supposing an aboriginal, instead of a lion, were the subject of the sketch—should we consider it an impossibility for that aboriginal to make such remarks in his own language as those suggested for the lion in the fable? Should we not feel that, at all events, he would be capable of doing so; while the lion could never, in the course of any number of centuries, or if he went through millions of evolutions, be brought to the point of conversing and reasoning and judging of artists and of works of art? Put any one of the brute creation you will in the lion's place, and your conviction will be the same—you will know that a brute beast has nothing mentally in common with yourself and never will have; whilst you at once detect, in the lowest savage, the presence of that mind by which, though he may be degraded, he becomes to you a brother.

It is attested by all writers of eminence that there is a community of nature throughout the human family. The lowest is cut off from the beast, and is unmistakably associated with the family of intelligent man. The man will, however low, be able to paint the lion; the lion, however high, will never be able to paint the man. Allow me to quote two unexceptional authorities as to the truth of this statement. Mr. Darwin himself says: "The Fuegians rank amongst the lowest barbarians; but I was continually struck with surprise how closely the three natives on board H. M. S. *Beagle*, who had lived some years in England and could talk a little English, resembled us in disposition, and in most of our mental qualities." Could not these "lowest barbarians," in their own way, have understood, and painted the man? Again: "The American aborigines, Negroes and Europeans, differ as much from each other in mind as any three races that can be named; yet I was incessantly struck, whilst living with the Fuegians on board the *Beagle*, with the many little traits of character, showing how similar their minds were to ours; and so it was with a full-blooded Negro with whom I happened once to be intimate." ("Voyage," vol. i, p. 232.) Then Mr. Tylor says: "The state of things amongst the lower tribes which presents itself to the student, is a *substantial similarity* in knowledge, arts and customs running through the whole world. Not that the culture of all tribes is alike —far from it; but if any art or custom belonging to a low tribe is selected at random, it is twenty to one that something substantially like it may be found in at least one place thousands of miles off, though it very frequently happens that there are large portions of the earth's surface lying between, where it has not been observed. Indeed, there are few things in crockery, clothing, arms, vessels, boots, ornaments, found in one place, that cannot be matched, more or less, nearly somewhere else." ("Researches," p. 169.)

Here, then, is a broad basis of oneness between all men, from a Newton or a Dante down to one of the aboriginals of Australia, or of the Terra del Fuego; and this is a basis or platform on which no animal or ape can possibly be invited to stand. The brute kingdom is one, the rational kingdom is another; they do not fuse or mingle; they are distinct and absolutely separated, not in degree alone, but in kind. "Mr. Wallace sees," says an able writer, "in the production of man the intervention of an external will. He remarks that the lowest types of savages are in possession of a brain, and of capacities far beyond any use to which they could apply them in their present condition, and that, therefore, they could not have been evolved from the mere necessities of their environments." They must, in one word, have been from the very first, of a different creation; and have been endowed with gifts and faculties which are never found, in ever so rudimentary a condition, amongst the animals of the field. Summing up his interesting investigation on this point, Mr. Mivart says: "We have found, as regards *language*, not only an essential agreement amongst all men, but even the dumb prove by their gestures that they are possessed of the really important part of the faculty, the *verbum mentale*. . . As to *morals*, we have found that not only are all races possessed of moral perception, but even that their fundamental moral principles are not in contradiction with our own. Concerning *Religion*, we have seen that religious conceptions appear to exist universally amongst all races of mankind. . . Respecting *community* of *nature*, we have been able to quote from Mr. Tylor assertions of the most unequivocal character." Now let our opponents, instead of bragging about their victory of Science, fill up the gulf, if they can, that thus separates brutes from men. Let them produce one single specimen of a brute that possesses the *verbum mentis* and expresses it by the *verbum oris;* that is, let them produce a brute animal who can converse, not like a parrot, but like a reasonable and reasoning being; let them produce before us a brute-beast who has some, ever so vague, idea of the moral law, or of the first principles of the barest morality, who knows the difference between duty and pleasure, and follows the former because conscience so dictates to it; let them produce us one single instance, amidst the myriads of brutes that have existed, or do exist, of one who seemed to entertain even the most nebulous and distant notion of Supreme Being, of a future state of reward and punishment, of prayer, praise, contrition, humility, or love; let them show one single example of community of intellectual nature between the man and the beast; let them exhibit to us the interesting sight of the lion painting the man, however roughly;—and then we will believe, not only that the gulf is not unbridgable, but we will earnestly maintain that in a very short space of time, the lion will cease to paint, and begin to tear the man to pieces. What, then, do we come to? Let me conclude in Mivart's words: "The final result therefore is that ethnology and archæology, though incapable of deciding as to the possibility of applying the monistic view (of man being one in kind with the brute) of evolution to man, yet, so far as they go, *oppose* that application. Thus the study of man past and present, by the last mentioned sciences, when used as a test of the adequacy of the *theory of evolution*, tends to show (though the ultimate decision, of course, rests with philosophy) that it is inadequate, and that another factor must be introduced, of which it declines to take any account—the action, namely, of a *Divine mind* as the direct and immediate originator and cause of the existence of its created image, the mind of man." ("Lessons from Nature," chap. vi., p. 166.)

Now, I ask you whether or not this study of the origin of man from a scientific stand-point has not landed us in just the very spot, away from which our opponents have been trying with all their skill to lead us? I ask you whether or no a "little" science is not a very dangerous thing? I ask you, as men of good will, whether or not, after what I have said, it is not reasonable, whether it does not satisfy your calm deliberate judgment, when I say that the tendency of Science is in the direction of man's spirituality, and goes to prove that he must have been the object of especial separate creation, rather than a being somehow or other evolved from a mud-fish or a protoplasm—a thing formed one knows not how, by mechanical force from carbon, hydrogen, oxygen and nitrogen? I put it to you which of the two theories seems shallow, which reasonable; which leaves you in bewilderment, and fills you with a sort of idea that some one is going mad; and which satisfies, as far as it goes, that intellectual creature which you call yourself, and makes you feel morally as well as intellectually satisfied and content, as one who, at all events, has a fairly good reason for the opinions which he holds, and cannot find as good reasons for any other?

I may here be asked how it is that scientific men can bring themselves to push before the public dangerous theories, and protest with a great flourish of trumpets that they are established facts, and are to be numbered among the great victories of science over ignorance and superstition? How is it they thus forget themselves, and their most grave responsibilities, when they cast doubt broadcast amongst the masses of the people, who cannot by any possibility, on account of their daily toil, and their want of training detect the poison and point out the lie? How is it that they have not more heart and feeling in them, than to impose upon the ignorant; and, in the name of that mysterious ogre "Science," stuff them with all manner of false notions about themselves, and lead them to darkness, degredation and despair? The reason is simple. Virchow, with very little circumlocution, has publicly given it to the world in his address to the great meeting of German Naturalists, referred to before. He feels it a solemn duty to warn his brother scientists upon the point; and thus, by implication, informs us how the plague is spreading, The fact is, scientific Atheists have like passions with their fellow-men. To quote a well known passage with the change of a single word:

"Hath not an Atheist eyes? hath not an Atheist hands, organs, dimensions, senses, affections, passions? fed with the same food, hurt with the same weapons, subject to the same diseases, healed by the same means, warmed and cooled by the same winter and summer, as a Christian is? If you prick them, do they not bleed? if you tickle them? do they not laugh? if you poison them, do they not die? if you wrong them, shall they not revenge?" ("Merchant of Venice," Act III.) Being thus like other men, some of them use their own especial weapons to gain their cherished ends. Hating Christianity and wishing to uproot its doctrines from their very foundations, they think to bring the crowbars of Natural Science to bear against it; and carried away by the eagerness of their passion, they are impatient of the excessively slow movements of Nature; are easily inclined to discover proofs and verifications where they are not to be found; and to come to hasty conclusions, from insufficient data, which are eventually upset by real scientific men, but which, for the moment, serve to bolster and support their peculiar views of like. It is evidently against this spirit, which is every day gaining ground and degrading Science, and bringing it into disrepute, that Virchow declaims, with such solemnity before the great meeting of men of science in Germany, when he says: "Every attempt to transform our problem into doctrines, to introduce our hypotheses as the bases of instruction—especially the attempt simply to dispossess the Church, and to supplant its dogmas forthwith by a religion of evolution—be assured, gentlemen, every such attempt will make shipwreck, and its wreck will also bring with it the greatest perils for the whole position of Science." Thus the bigots of Science are preparing for the downfall of the study they love not wisely, but too well. Let calm men of genuine Science continue their laborious and indefatigable inquiry; let them carefully verify their data; let them keep passion, prejudice and pride at bay; let them remember that they are *men;* and there is not the slightest doubt that they will not only, by their discoveries, be entitled to the proud title of benefactors of mankind, but that they will also furnish, without their caring, or perhaps wishing, to do so, innumerable new evidences to the philosopher of the truth of those great fundamental positions on which the fabric of Religion rests.

Having now led you into view of the great truth that man was created by God, and that he possesses faculties and endowments which indicate a destiny higher than that of the irrational brute; having suggested to you that Science, so far as it does point to anything, points towards the Christian view of man's origin and destiny; having steadily and slowly, though I trust securely, led you along towards the rational explanation of the enigma of human life, and towards those positions which are directly connected with the dogmas of the Christian religion;—I will now leave you to yourselves to ponder over what I have been saying; and whilst doing so, allow me to suggest to you to look into your own interior soul, and ask yourself if you are not as spontaneously conscious that a brute animal, when you come in contact with it, has no point of moral or intellectual oneness with you, as you are, when you meet a fellow man, that with him there is at once a community of mind and heart. From the one you feel estranged, as you would from an automaton; in the other you at once perceive a likeness to yourself. Again, look into your spirits, and look up to heaven, and ask yourselves whether or not there be within you a something which silently suggests that you are more than a brute, the mere growth of a molecule; and that you are, on the contrary, so made that you feel yourself fitted or fit to be fitted for a higher and more spiritual world than this. Ask yourself if the following lines—a free translation from a Latin ode by Pope—not an ode written by a Christian, but by one who had the yearnings of our common humanity in' him—ask yourselves if you could reasonably believe that a mere piece of carbon could be so acted on by material forces as to produce a soul capable of uttering the following cry, and of forecasting this vision of the future :—

> Vital spark of heavenly flame !
> Quit, oh, quit this mortal frame !
> Trembling, hoping, ling'ring, flying ;
> Oh, the pain, the bliss of dying !
> Cease, fond Nature, cease thy strife,
> And let me languish into life !
>
> Hark ! they whisper—angels say,
> " Sister spirit, come away ! "
> What is this absorbs me quite ;
> Steals my senses, shuts my sight,
> Drowns my spirits, draws my breath ?
> Tell me, my soul, can this be death ?
>
> The world recedes, it disappears ;
> Heaven opens to my eyes !—my ears,
>   With sounds seraphic ring :
> Lend, lend your wings ! I mount ! I fly !
> O, Grave ! where is thy victory ?
>   O, Death ! where is thy sting ?

Next Sunday I shall treat of several weighty questions regarding the Divine Being, the Creator and Governor of all ; and taking man as he stands before you, just as I have represented him, showing his relations to God and God's dealings with him, appealing to Science and Philosophy in furtherance of my thesis, I shall, so far it is in me to deal with such momentous questions, give you sufficient reason for holding with certainty not merely that God exists, but, moreover, that God is the Master of man, and his Creator ; One who alone is capable of satisfying that deep cry of his soul which represents the voice of his entire being—the voice of the finite creature acknowledging his dependence on that Infinite God who made him, out of whose Hands he came, and into whose Hands he will return. Admit man, as I have described him, and it is shallowness, as well as bad logic to deny a God; whilst, on the other hand, it becomes highly reasonable to declare His existence, His Providence, and His love.

GOD.

On Sunday evening, March 23, when His Grace, Archbishop Roger Bede Vaughan, delivered his third Lenten address at St. Mary's Pro-cathedral, Sydney, Australia, there was even a larger attendance than on the preceding evening. The subject of the discourse was "God." His Grace said:

"Last Sunday evening I did what I could to lead you to the threshold of the great truth regarding man's intimate communication with God, on which so much depends in the Christian scheme. I showed you, by means of several arguments, that man differs radically and in kind from brute beasts; that this fundamental difference springs from his spiritual nature; and that that nature is so fashioned that it spontaneously tends towards something higher, purer more perfect than itself. I pointed out the fact that man is essentially religious; and that he possesses a moral no less than an intellectual nature; and that his intellect, his reason and his heart, all three, point with a straight finger towards this profound and universally-received conclusion, namely, that the very fact of man existing as man, leads on to a reasonable belief in a Personal God, a Creator and a Sovereign Ruler of the Universe.

Having thus carried my reasoning along so far, it now remains for me to complete the train of thought with which I began; and to unfold before the eye of your intellect those positions which show how the mind of man comes into communication with that of God, and which tend towards proving that not only does man yearn and hold out the hands of his soul towards his Maker, but that the same Maker in return enters into communication with His creature, and offers him sufficient motives for believing, with an absolute and sovereign certainty, in His existence as a Personal, All-holy and All-wise Creator. And it is quite necessary to insist upon this great primary truth with all the earnestness and all the argument at our command; for, in the present age, when the very foundations of religion are scanned anew and tested; when men feel as little remorse in denying the existence of God as they do in denying the existence of the man in the moon; when no dogma, however sacred or venerable, is treated with the slightest reverence or respect, but all have to be put in the witness-box and bullied and brow-beaten by the brazen, self-sufficient votaries of a Negative religion; when nothing is safe from narrow brains and profane hands and tongues, from the worry of a shallow philosophy; in such a condition of affairs as this, it is absolutely necessary to meet our opponents with boldness as well as logic, and to state, in the most unmistakable terms, the thesis which we are combatting, and the thesis, on the other hand, that we have undertaken to defend.

Allow me, therefore, to state the thesis that I am joining issue on, as drawn out by one of the ablest philosophers belonging to the Religion of Denial, so that there may be no misunderstanding regarding the intellectual position assumed by our opponents—no doubt as to the opponents with whom we are contending, and as to the character of that doctrine which they are endeavoring to push amongst the people. "Inexorable logic," says this exponent of the Religion of Denial, "has forced us to conclude that, viewing the question as to the existence of God only by the light which modern science has shed upon it, there no longer appears to be any semblance of an argument in its favor. There can be no longer any more doubt that the existence of God is wholly unnecessary to explain any of the phenomena of the universe, than there is a doubt that if I leave go (sic) of my pen it will fall to the table. . . . The knowledge that a Deity is superfluous, as an explanation of anything, being grounded on the doctrine of the persistence of force, is grounded on an *a priori* necessity of reason, *i. e.*, if this fact were not so our science, our thought, our very existence itself would be scientifically impossible." ("A Candid Examination of Theism by Physicus," p. 64.)

Here, then, is a categorical and clear statement opposing a primary truth of Christianity. Here the existence of God is denied boldly and without circumlocution, whilst it is asserted, moreover, that did God exist man could not exist; that "our science, our thought, our very existence itself would be scientifically impossible." We could not possibly find or invent a thesis more antagonistically opposed to our own contention. Our adversaries say that if God existed man could not possibly live, or move or have any being; we contend the reverse; that if man exists, as was explained last Sunday, possessing the gifts and faculties which I then ascribed to him, that if such be the case God does exist, and can be shown to every rational creature, by means of sufficient proof, to be the Personal God and the Creator of the Universe. True, we should prefer by far to be allowed to love and adore our Master in peace; but the world will not let us; there is a propaganda of Denial around us; and we must, therefore, rouse ourselves up, and, however grating to the feelings, enter into the arena with our opponents, and defend, with the weapons of logic and philosophy, the great primary truth of our religious teachings.

"It is hard," says Janet, "to see the noblest beliefs of humanity weighed in the balance of a subtle dialectic. Of what use is philosophy, we are asked, but to observe what is clear, and to shake what is defended? It has been thought by some a sufficient praise of such spiritualistic philosophy to say, It does not hinder us from believing in God. In this order of ideas, it seems that demonstration weakens rather than proves, affords more doubt than light, and teaches us to dispute rather than to decide. We are sensible," continues Janet, "as any of this anxiety and trouble; and the fact mentioned, which is nothing but the truth, is one of the proofs of the feebleness of the human mind. But it is also precisely part of the greatness of the human mind to learn to consider vigorously and calmly its natural condition, and courageously to seek to remedy it. We distinguish, for our part, even in the order of Nature, two things,—Faith and Science, the object of the one being to supplement the other. There is a natural, practical and moral faith in the existence of a Deity, which no demonstration can equal, to which no reasoning is adequate. 'A single sigh towards the future and the better,' it is admirably said by Hemsterhuys, 'is more than geometrical demonstration of the Deity.' But, if the soul needs to believe, it also needs to know; it will try to unfold the causes of things by the laws of reason; and it is one of the strongest temptations of the human mind to equalize its knowledge with its faith, *fides quærens intellectum.* Hence the necessity of applying the abstract and discursive methods of science to what it would seem ought only to be an object of love and hope. . . As a philosopher, I am bound to but one thing,—to admit as true what appears to me evident, nothing more. That there should·be a very great difference between the demonstrations of Science and the instincts of Faith is self-evident; for an adequate demonstration of the Deity, of His existence and essence, would imply a reason adequate thereto. The absolute reason can alone know the absolute being as he is. If, then, Faith, anticipating this impossible knowledge, gives us moral certainty, Science can only give a relative approximate knowledge, subject to revision in another state of knowledge, but which, for us, is the mode of representation the most adequate to which we could attain. When Bacon says that we only know God by a refracted ray (*radio refracto*,) this expression, admired by all; just means that the idea we have of Him is inadequate, without, however, being untrue, as the projection of a circle is not a circle, although it faithfully reproduces all its parts." ("Final Causes," book ii, p. 319.)

Let me now enter into this most important subject, on which the great fabric of our Arguments so much depends, —the existence of God. I will bring before your notice the two principal proofs which have been the solace and satisfaction of every character of mind in every age of the world,—the proof from the world without you and the proof drawn from the world within. I will then proceed to present to your consideration the united force of the illumination and evidence in support of this thesis, which, it appears to me, bears with such irresistible pressure upon the whole of one's being as a man, that it is impossible to resist its conclusiveness without doing violence to the deepest instincts and highest faculties of one's nature. Before, however, entering on the proof drawn from the external world, allow me to observe that the weight of its testimony comes all the more powerfully on the mind if some simple and intelligible object is examined which lies within the range of easy observation. Take, for example, out of the myriad objects we could select, the eye and the voice of man; and, from their examination, you may infer what must be the skill, wisdom and resource of Him who created the whole universe, supports it, and orders it according to established law. Indeed, the more minute the object scrutinized, so much the more cause for wonder does it present; a universe or a drop of water equally witnesses to evidences of design surpassing the power and intelligence of man. Now, take the case of the human eye. "In the construction of this organ," says Trendelenburg, "we must either admit that light has triumphed over matter and has fashioned it, or else it is the matter itself which has become the master of the light. This is at least what should result from the law of efficient causes, but neither the one or the other of these two hypotheses takes place in reality. No ray of light falls within the secret depths of the maternal womb, where the eye is formed. Still less could inert matter, which is nothing without the energy of light, be capable of comprehending it. Yet the light and the eye are made the one for the other, and in the miracle of the eye resides the latent consciousness of the light. The moving cause, with its necessary development, is here employed for a higher service. The end commands the whole, and watches over the execution of the parts; and it is with the aid of the end that the eye becomes 'the light of the body.'" ("Logische Untersuchungen," tom. ii, chap. ix, p. 4.) Even the supposed imperfections of the eye are, in reality, advantageous. "The appropriateness of the eye," says Helmholtz, "to its end exists in the most perfect manner, and is revealed even in the limit given to its defects. A reasonable man will not take a razor to cleave blocks; in like manner, every useless refinement in the optical use of the eye would have rendered that organ more delicate and slower in its application." ("Revue des cours publics scientifiques," 1re serie, t. vi, p. 219.)

Now take the voice of man. "In studying the voice of man," says Muller, "one is struck with the infinite art with which the organ which produces it is constructed. No instrument of music is at all comparable to this; for organs and pianos, despite all their resources, are imperfect in other respects. Some of these instruments, like mouth-pipes, do not permit us to pass from piano to forte; in others, as in all those which are played by percussion, there are no means of maintaining the sound. The organ has two registers,—that of the mouth-pipes and that of the reed-pipes,—in this point of view resembling the human voice, with its chest register and falsetto. But none of these instruments combines all advantages like the human voice. The vocal organ has, above them all, the advantage of being able to give all the sounds of the musical scale, and all their shades, with a single mouth-pipe, while the most perfect of reed-instruments requires a separate pipe for each sound.". ("Manual," tom. ii, chap. ii, p. 197.)

Now, permit me to bring before your notice the arguments of men of great ability, of high education, of diverse mind and bias, and living in various ages of the world, in support of my thesis based upon such marks of design as these.

"If one were to find on a desert island," says Fenelon, "a beautiful marble statue, he would doubtless at once say: There have formerly been men here; I reconize the hand of a talented sculptor." "These words," says Janet, "have had in recent times a curious justification. What has been found, not in a desert island, but in antediluvian deposits, is not marble statues, nor magnificent palaces, but tools, and the rudest, possible, hatchet as at least is supposed, stones cut in an awkward manner, such as can even sometimes be met with when rocks are broken. And yet, however rude this work may be, the fact that such stones have been met with in great numbers has sufficed to the conclusion that they cannot be a freak of Nature. That mass of objects collected in the same place, cut in the same manner, indicates a relation of finality; they are no larger stones, they are *instruments*—that is to say, objects *destined* to cut, to pierce, to strike, to produce this or that effect. This induction does not raise the shadow of a doubt, and yet, if a coincidence of unknown causes has been able to produce the wing of the bird so marvellously adapted for flying, why should not another coincidence of unknown causes have been able to produce this heap of rude stones, so imperfectly adapted to their object?" ("Final Causes," book 1, chap. i., p. 30.)

So far for Fenelon, the Catholic philosopher; now turn in quite another direction. Open the profoundest of Moliere's comedies (" Le festin de Pierre," act 3, scene 1), and you will hear the good Sganarelle draw out one of the most powerful evidences regarding a Supreme Being, and one of the most ancient that has ever impressed the mind of the philosopher. In trying to convert the unbelieving Don Juan, he says to him : " I have not studied like you, thank God, and no one could boast of having ever taught me anything ; but with my small sense, my small judgment, I see things better than books and understand very well that this world that we see is not a mushroom that has come of itself in a night. I would ask you—Who has made these trees, these rocks, this earth, and yonder sky above? and whether all that has made itself. . . . Can you see all the inventions of which the human machine is composed, without admiring the way in which it is arranged, one part

with another—these nerves, bones, veins, arteries, these
. . . lungs, this heart, this liver, and all these other
ingredients that are there, and that . . ? My reasoning is that there is something wonderful in man, whatever you may say, and which all the savants cannot explain." Though put into the mouth of a valet, this great argument was handled at Athens ages ago by the clear and logical mind of Socrates, Fenelon develops it in his beautiful treatise on the "Existence of God," and whilst Cicero has handled the same subject from a Pagan standpoint in his *De Natura Deorum*, and Kant can never criticise it without treating it, especially as developed by the French divine, with the most respectful sympathy.

So far for Moliere. Let us now take a renowned mathematician and astronomer, I refer to the illustrious Kepler. This great thinker was one of those chosen scientific men whose minds seem to expand with religious feeling in proportion as they advance in the course of scientific discovery. The realm of Science with him not only harmonized with, but witnessed to the kingdom of Religion. He, like most thinkers of his day, engaged his keen and powerful intellect in trying to solve the theory of atoms and their combinations. He passed many days together in such meditations as these· On one occasion, after he had been engaged for many hours in endeavoring to solve the great problem, the dinner-bell rang; and having sat down to table with [Barbara, his wife, the salad was put upon the table. With his mind full of the subject of his meditations, and feeling that there was, after all, but one reasonable way for accounting for the order, and beauty, and oneness, yet variety, of the world spread out beneath his feet, he suddenly stopped eating and said to his wife: "Dost think," said he, "that if from the creation plates of tin, leaves of lettuce, grains of salt, drops of oil and vinegar, and fragments of hard-boiled eggs were floating in space in all directions and without order, chance could assemble them to-day to form a salad?" "Certainly not so good a one," she replied, "nor so well seasoned as this!" (See Bertrand, "Les fondateurs de l'astronomie moderne," p. 154.)

Evidently, the profoundest thought of the great astronomer, and the natural light of reason in a woman's mind, led straight to one distinct conclusion.

Now, leave the profound philosopher and the woman, and take a little child, and see how his mind would be affected. Let me select, however, an intelligent child, the son of a keen Scotch philosopher. I refer to Beattie. This able man had a boy, and when the child was between five and six years of age, in fact, just arriving at the use of reason, his father was anxious to instruct him in religion, and bring before his opening intelligence the fact of the existence of God. The canny Scotchman thought of a clever expedient for bringing home to the child's mind the great truth on which all happiness is based. He went one day quietly to the child's little garden, and sowed some mustard-and-cress seed there, and so disposed of it that it should, when grown up, exhibit the three initial letters of the child's name. But to give the account in the father's words: "Ten days after," says Beattie, "the child came running to me all amazed, and told me that his name had grown in the garden. I smiled at these words, and appeared not to attach much importance to what he had said. But he insisted on taking me to see what had happened. 'Yes,' said I, in coming to the place, 'I see well enough that it is so; but there is nothing wonderful in this, it is a mere accident,' and went away. But he followed me, and, walking beside me, said very seriously: 'That cannot be an accident. Some one must have prepared the seed, to produce this result.' Perhaps these were not his very words, but this was the substance of his thought. 'You think, then,' said I to him, 'that what here appears as regular as the letters of your name, cannot be produced by chance?' 'Yes,' he said firmly, 'I think so.' 'Well, then, look at yourself, consider your hands and fingers, your legs and feet, and all your members, and do they not seem to you regular in their appearance, and useful in their service?' 'Doubtless they do.' 'Can they, then, be the result of chance?' 'No,' replied he, 'that cannot be; some one must have made me them.' 'And who is that some one?' I asked him. He replied that he did not know. I then made known to him the name of the great Being who made all the world, and regarding His Nature I gave him all the instruction adapted to his age. The lesson struck him so profoundly, that he has never forgotten either it or the circumstance that was the occasion of it."

Now let us shift the scene again; let us leave the pure atmosphere of Beattie's home, and plunge for a moment, in imagination, into the brilliant and depraved society of Parisian Atheists, who, in the days when Atheism was rampant in France, frequented the drawing-room of Baron d'Holbach. One of the frequenters of that drawing-room and society, the Abbe Galiani, was one of the most gifted of the clergy of that day, and renowned through society as a remarkably witty improvisatore. But I will allow Abbe Morellet to give his own version of the matter. "After dinner and coffee," says Morellet, "the Abbe sits down in an arm-chair, his legs crossed like a tailor, as was his custom, and, it being warm, he takes his wig in one hand, and, gesticulating with the other, commences nearly as follows: 'I will suppose, gentlemen, that he among you who is most fully convinced that the world is the effect of chance, is playing with three dice, I do not say in a gambling-house, but in the best house in Paris—his antagonist throws sixes once, twice, thrice, four times—in a word, constantly. However short the duration of the game, my friend Diderot, thus losing his money, will unhesitatingly say, without a moment's doubt, "The dice are loaded; this is a gambling-house!" What, then, philosopher? Because ten or a dozen throws of the dice have emerged from the box so as to make you lose six francs, you believe firmly that this is in consequence of an adroit manœuvre, an artificial combination, a well-planned roguery; and yet seeing in this universe so prodigious a number of combinations, thousands of times more difficult and complicated, more sustained and useful, etc., do you not recognize the skill and intelligence of Him in whose hands are the end of the earth, and who has ordered all things in number, in weight and measure?'" Fenelon the Catholic Divine, Tillotson the Protestant, and Cicero the Pagan orator and philosopher, are convinced by, and make use of the same character of proof. Possibly, Fenelon borrowed much of his Treaties from the *De Natura Deorum;* anyhow, both he and Cicero, to show the absurdity of the supposition that the world came together by a fortuitous concourse of atoms, ask the pertinent question whether the throwing of four-and-twenty letters of the alphabet together would ever result in the formation of one single verse of the *Iliad?*

While Tillotson asks, "If twenty thousand blind men were to set out from different places in England remote from each other, what chance would there be that they would end by meeting, all arranged in a row, upon Salisbury Plain?" Kant, the great German philospher, who perhaps has exerted a greater sway over English thought than any other modern thinker, throws his proofs of God's existence and unity into a four-fold division in the following order: first, he maintains, there is everywhere in the world manifest signs of an order regulated by design; secondly, this harmonious order does not necessarily belong to the things of the world, but only contingently, that is, it must have been produced *ab extra*, from outside; thirdly, therefore, there must exist one sublime wise cause, which must have produced the world as an Omnipotent Being, not acting blindly, but freely and intelligently; and, finally, and fourthly, he deduces the unity of this cause from that of the relations of the parts of the world looked upon as the different pieces of a work of art. Janet shows, with great clearness of illustration, what we should have to admit did we refuse to admit the existence of an intelligent Creator. "If the element of things," he says, "be conceived as mobile atoms, moving in all possible directions, and ending by lighting on such a happy combination as results in a planetary globe, a solar system, or an organized body, it will have to be said as well that it is in virtue of a happy combination that the atoms have ended by taking the form of a human brain, which, by the mere fact of that combination, became fit for thought. Now what is this but to say that letters thrown haphazard might form the *Iliad* in their successive throws, since the *Iliad* itself is only one of the phenomena produced by the thinking activity? But the human mind, whether in the arts or in the sciences, has produced, and will produce, similar phenomena without end. It would not then be a single verse, a single poem, it would be all thought, with all its poems, and all its inventions, which would be the result of a happy throw." ("Final Causes," book i, chap. v, p. 152.)

Let us now turn to the proofs of God's existence from the world within, and I begin by bringing before you the the views of one of the most subtle thinkers of the present age, and one of the most conscientious; a man who has passed a long life in the consideration of the gravest religious problems. I refer to Dr. Newman, of the London Oratory. Fortunately, in his "Apologia," he has been, through accident, forced, if I may so speak, to make his interior mind and spirit known, as it otherwise never would have been. There are two remarkable and profound observations regarding his view of the existence of God, in the "Apologia;" and in the "Grammar of Assent" he draws out, what evidently for him is the most cogent proof amongst so many of the Theist's Doctrine. In his early youth he said he was led to "rest in the thought of two and two only absolute and luminously self-evident beings, himself and his Creator." ("Apologia," p. 4.) "Of all points of faith," he says further on, "the being of a God is, to my apprehension, encompassed with most difficulty, and yet borne in upon our minds with most power." Further on again: "Starting, then, with the being of a God (which, as I have said, is as certain to me as the certainty of my own existence, though when I try to put the grounds of that certainty into logical shape, I find a difficulty in doing so in the mood and figure to my satisfaction), I look out of myself into the world of men." (Ibid, p. 241.) In the "Grammar of Assent" he dedicates a section to show how man gives a real assent to the existence of God. He says: "What I am directly aiming at, is to explain how we gain an image of God and give a real assent to the proposition that He exists. And next, in order to do this, of course I must start from some first principle—and that first principle, which I assume, and shall not attempt to

prove, is that we have naturally a conscience. . . . .
This being taken for granted, I shall attempt to show that in this special feeling, which follows on the commission of what we call right and wrong, lie the materials for the real apprehension of a Divine Sovereign Judge. . . . .
If, as is the case, we feel responsibility, are ashamed, are frightened, at transgressing the voice of conscience, this implies that there is One to whom we are responsible, before whom we are ashamed, whose claims upon us we fear. If, on doing wrong, we feel the same tearful, broken-hearted sorrow which overwhelms us on hurting a mother; if, on doing right, we enjoy the same sunny serenity of mind, the same soothing, satisfactory delight which follows on our receiving praise from a father, we certainly have within us the image of some person, to whom our love and veneration look, in whose smile we find our happiness, for whom we yearn, towards whom we direct our pleadings, in whose anger we are troubled and waste away. These feelings in us are such as require for their exciting cause an intelligent being; we are not affectionate towards a stone, nor do we feel shame before a horse or dog; we have no remorse or compunction on breaking mere human law; yet, so it is, conscience excites all these painful emotions, confusion, forboding, self-condemnation; and, on the other hand, it sheds upon us a deep peace, a sense of security, a resignation, and a hope, which there is no sensible, no earthly object to elicit. 'The wicked flees, when no one pursueth,' then why does he flee? whence his terror? Who is it that he sees in solitude, in darkness, in the hidden chambers of his heart? If the cause of these emotions does not belong to this visible world, the Object to which his perception is directed must be Supernatural and Divine; and thus the phenomena of conscience, as a dictate, avail to

impress the imagination with the picture of a Supreme Governor, a Judge, holy, just, powerful, all-seeing, retributive, and is the creative principle of Religion, as the moral sense is the principle of Ethics." ("Grammar of Assent," p. 106.)

Here is the great argument and proof or witness to the existence of a Personal God, which has not only so deeply pressed in upon the mind of John Henry Newman, but that it may be said to have been the mainspring of all the greatness and the heroism of the saints. Their actual lives, the labors and sufferings, the martyrdoms and deaths, the heart-sacrifices and life-long self-oblations of them, which we read of in their annals, all down the ages, from the first till now—these overwhelming practical testimonies, to their intense convictions, tend to impress the mind with some sort of notion of the force with which the intuitions of their conscience came home to their spirits. Even in the earliest days of childhood, this voice in the soul, witnessing to a higher Being than man himself, produces an effect, which remains after the child has grown to manhood, and can look back upon his past personal history, and analyze the feelings of his heart. These impressions are beautifully brought out by Henry Vaughan, when he says:

> Happy those early days, when I
> Shined in my Angel infancy;
> * * * *
> Before I taught my tongue to wound
> My conscience with a sinful sound:
> Or had the black art to dispense
> A several sin to every sense;
> But felt through all this fleshly dress
> Bright shoots of everlastingness.

So far for Dr. Newman regarding the existence of God.

I must now beg of you to place yourselves in very different company—in the company of one of as different an intellectual make from Newman as well could be conceived—in the company of David Hume, the sceptic *par excellence*. That Hume would search out every possible objection to the doctrine of God's existence and man's motives for believing in it as he does, is inevitable, when we consider the bias and the build of Hume's mind. He stands out as affording one of the most remarkable instances of the deep truth contained in the utterance of Dr. Newman, when he says that whilst the existence of God is a luminous and self-evident truth, of which he feels as certain as of his own existence, that whilst that truth is "borne in upon our minds with most power," still "it is encompassed with most difficulty." Like all great fundamental propositions, this one, though-relentless in the grasp with which it seizes and holds the mind prisoner; still, that same mind which, through its very constitution, is here compelled to give an absolute assent, on account of its limited calibre, is incapable of explaining every difficulty away. Now, David Hume did all that human ingenuity could possibly do to discover difficulties, and marshal them to the very best advantage. He was not a man to accept any proposition that he was not forced to accept through the sheer pressure of evidence, or through that bright illumination which springs from a primary truth. As for his difficulties, those are known to most persons who have studied his works. My question is: What was the decision he came to in spite of such difficulties? What is his distinct teaching representing the residue of his thought, after he had skimmed away whatever he considered untenable through the pressure of arguments appealing from the opposite side?

But before I place his conclusion before you, permit me

to make one short digression which will explain his position, and account for the fact that a man may firmly believe a thing, and yet be conscious of the difficulties which are connected with that belief—that a man may possess that iron grasp on truth which would make him a ready martyr, and yet be absolutely unable to explain away every difficulty that presented itself, as accompanying that absolute conviction. To my mind one of the most useful and luminous utterances ever given forth by Dr. Newman is contained in the following passage from the "Apologia"— "Many persons," he says, "are very sensitive of the difficulties of Religion; I am as sensitive of them as any one; but I have never been able to see a connection between apprehending those difficulties, however keenly, and multiplying them to any extent, and on the other hand doubting the doctrines to which they are attached. *Ten thousand difficulties do not make one doubt*, as I understand the subject; difficulty and doubt are incommensurate. There of course may be difficulties in the evidence; but I am speaking of difficulties intrinsic to the doctrines themselves, or as to their relations with each other. A man may be annoyed that he cannot work out a mathematical problem, of which the answer is or is not given to him, without doubting that it admits of an answer, or that a certain particular answer is the true one." Then he continues, "Of all the points of faith, the being of a God is, to my own apprehension, encompassed with most difficulty, and yet is borne in upon our minds with most power." ("Apologia," chap. v., p. 238.)

Now after exhausting all his difficulties and marshaling them against the proofs we possess, or reasons we have for believing in the existence of God, Hume still publishes to the world in his "Natural History of Religion," (1757,) the following conclusions, which become excessively valuable when the character of the writer's mind, and his strong bias in the opposite direction, are taken into account. He says:

"The whole frame of Nature bespeaks an Intelligent Author; and no rational inquirer can, *after serious reflection, suspend his belief for a moment* with regard to the primary principle of genuine Theism and Religion." . . . "Were men led into the apprehension of invisible, intelligent power, by a contemplation of the works of Nature, they could never possibly entertain any conception but of one single Being, who bestowed existence and order in this vast machine, and adjusted all its parts according to one regular plan or connected system. For though, to persons of a certain turn of mind it may not appear altogether absurd, that several independent beings, endowed with superior wisdom, might conspire in the contrivance and execution of one regular plan, yet is this a merely arbitrary supposition, which, even if allowed posssible, must be confessed neither to be supported by probability nor necessity. All things in the universe are evidently of a piece. Everything is adjusted to everything. One design prevails throughout the whole. And this uniformity leads the mind to acknowledge one Author; because the conception of different authors, without any distinction of attributes or operations, serves only to give perplexity to the imagination, without bestowing any satisfaction on the understanding." ("Natural History of Religion," iv., 435, 442.)

Philo is made, in Hume's "Dialogues," to finish thus: "If the whole of Natural Theology, as some people seem to maintain, resolves itself into one simple, though somewhat ambiguous, at least undefined proposition—That the cause or causes of order in the universe probably bear some remote analogy to human intelligence; if this proposition be not capable of extension, variation, or more particular explication; if it affords no inference that affects human life, or can be the source of any action or forbearance; and if the analogy, imperfect as it is, can be carried no further than to the human intelligence, and cannot be transferred, with any appearance of probability, to the other qualities of the mind; if this really be the case, what can the most inquisitive, contemplative, and religious man do more than give a plain, philosophical assent to the proposition, as it occurs, and believe that the arguments on which it is established exceed the objections which lie against it? Some astonishment indeed will naturally arise from the greatness of the object; some melancholy from its obscurity; some contempt of human reason, that it can give no solution more satisfactory with regard to so extraordinary and magnificent a question. But believe me, Cleanthes, the most natural sentiment which a well-disposed mind will feel on this occasion, is a longing desire and expectation that heaven would please to dissipate, at least alleviate, this profound ignorance, by affording some more particular revelation to mankind, and making discoveries of the nature, attributes and operations of the Divine Object of our faith." ("Dialogues," ii., p. 547-8.) Finally, Philo, whilst, in the "Dialogues," pushing Scepticism to its utmost limits, is compelled to say, in spite of the mass of objections urged the other way, that "where reasonable men"—to whom alone I am addressing myself—"treat these subjects, the question can never be concerning the *Being* but only the *Nature* of the Deity. The former truth, as you will observe, *is unquestionable and self-evident*. Nothing exists without a cause, and the original Cause of this universe. . . we call God, and piously ascribe to Him every species of perfection." (Ibid. ii., p. 439).

It was the light of the self-evident truth in the conscience of Kirkman that made him exclaim, with as deed a philosophy as feeling: "Through the Infinite I cannot think; but upwards, still upwards, towards it my soul can soar, scorning the finite. That Infinite scientifically I cannot know; but the Infinite is my cause. Believing and adoring, I affirm Him with a boldness and a conviction surpassing all that I can feel or utter on my themes of finite science. My Cause lives—the infinite Life. My Cause thinks, knows and works—the infinite Intuition, Counsel, and Energy works in the full harmony of victorious science in every point and line of force, in every throb of consciousness, never absent nor forgetting, never pausing nor weary. And my Cause loves—the infinite Love." ("Philosophy without Assumptions," p. 262).

Again: "Now, if the child, when he becomes a man, should ask himself, 'What are those wondrous workings?' may he not be pardoned if, despising the dogmas of mock science, and reasoning only from what he knows, he compares these energies with the only force of which he is master—his own will-force? . . . What can balance will but will? What can be measured by will but will? What can combine and harmonize with will but will? What can have equivalence and real relation in thought and act to will but will? When a man has dared to doubt, and, doubting, to think boldly up to this point, you might as well beseech this stone, falling freely, not to rush towards the earth's centre, as try to prevent that soul from bursting out, like the smitten unbeliever in Bethel. 'Surely God is in this place, and I knew it not.' I glory in believing that all those forces are manifestations of the conscious present working will of the God in whom I live and move and have my being—F—O—R—C—E spells WILL." ("Philosophy without Assumptions," p. 263.

Now let us pause for a few minutes, and add up what we have already done. I have brought before your notice the clear statements, absolute convictions of a first-class Catholic theologian, Fenelon; of a renowned French comic writer, Moliere; of a profound German metaphysician, Kant; of an astronomer and mathematician of world-wide reputation, Kepler; of a clerical wit in the Abbe Galiani; of an able Anglican divine in Tillotson; of the first of Roman orators, Cicero; of the keenest of Greek thinkers, Socrates; of an able modern thinker, Kirkman; of John Henry Newman, the Catholic philosopher; and of the sceptic, David Hume. All these men—men of keenest faculties, sharpened up to the highest pitch, all of them profound thinkers—came to the distinct and absolute conclusion that the fact of the existence of God is a self-evident truth, which through the very force of its witness, in spite of all difficulties, they were compelled to give their absolute and unqualified assent to. Now, could you imagine any possible subject of primary importance relating to religion on which every one of these men would perfectly and absolutely agree, declaring it to be a self-evident truth, and that they should turn out, after all, to have been absolutely wrong, and their assertion absolutely false? Could you imagine those men, without having had any communication with each other, Pagan, Catholic, Protestant, Sceptic, all fixing upon one religious proposition, and declaring it, after profound study, to be incontrovertibly and self-evidently true, and for it afterwards to turn out to be unquestionably and absolutely the reverse; that what they declared, and one and all protested to have seen with their own eyes, had never been seen by any single one of them? Would not any reasonable man, without going into their arguments or proofs, if he were certain that they had studied the matter to their best ability, feel that he would be acting reasonably in coming to the conclusion that what they all so firmly fixed upon as self-evident and unquestionable would have, at all events, reasonable evidence in its support? That what they declared so stoutly they saw with their own eyes, they did see with those eyes of theirs? And if to these asseverations were added the *consensus* of all mankind, in every age and clime, with the exception of perhaps a handful who professed not to see, would it not be reasonable to adhere to this practically unanimous declaration of humanity, and to consider that, in this case, the *Vox Populi* was the *Vox Dei*? And if by chance you did not see so clearly as they, would it not be prudent and wise to turn your eyes towards yourself, and find out whether or not vice had obscured your vision? whether you had not, perhaps, abused the nature God had given you, and crippled or drugged your faculties so as to impair their use?

But how comes it that there is this moral *consensus* of mankind to the fact of that existence of God; and that the very child feels no difficulty, accepts, as a matter of course, this momentous truth? It is because God gives His "light" to every man born into this world; because each has the *sensus numinis*, or an internal conviction, when he analyzes his conscience and his moral nature, that God does exist. It is a truth that shines with the brilliancy of its own light, and all the arguments and proofs brought forward do not so much establish it as new, as confirm the previous profound conviction, and add cumulative evidence to that intense persuasion that lives within the conscience. There is no other adequate way of accounting for the luminous intensity and universality of this intellectual asseveration, in spite of the profound mysteries and multitudinous difficulties with which it is encompassed as by a fog. Allow me to read to you the words of as learned and scientific a German professor as ever ornamented the University of Oxford—I mean Professor Max Muller. He, from his standpoint, explains the *sensus numinis* with great felicity. "As soon as a man becomes conscious of himself," he says, "as soon as he perceives himself as distinct from all other things and persons, he at the same time becomes conscious of a Higher Self, a higher power, without which neither he nor anything else would have any life or reality. We are so fashioned, and it is no merit of ours, that we feel on all sides our dependence on something else, and all nations join in some way or other in the words of the Psalmist, 'He that hath made us and not we ourselves.' This is the first sense of the Godhead, the *sensus numinis* as it has been called; for it is a *sensus*, an immediate perception, not the result of reasoning or generalization, but an intuition as irresistible as the impression of our senses. This *sensus numinis*, or, as we may call it in more homely language, faith, is the source of all religion; it is that without which no religion, either good or bad, is possible." ("Lectures on the Science of Language," second series, p. 436.)

Let us look at this universality of conviction regarding the Almighty. Let me take an example on a large scale of the *sensus numinis* in one of the most venerable people, and by far one of the most cultured that ever lived. I refer to the ancient Egyptians. Thousands of years ago, filled with the intimate sense of the existence and power of

the Almighty God, that people poured forth their hearts in
the following joyous hymn of praise to the Creator:

Hail to Thee, say all creatures;
Salutation from every land;
To the height of Heaven, to the breadth of the earth;
To the depths of the sea;
The gods adore Thy Majesty.
The spirits Thou hast made exalt Thee,
Rejoicing before the feet of their begetter.
They cry out welcome to Thee,
Father of the father of all the gods;
Who raises the heavens, who fixes the earth.
Maker of beings, Creator of existences,
Sovereign of life, health and strength, Chief of the gods;
We worship Thy spirit *who alone* hast made us;
We, whom Thou hast made, thank Thee, that Thou hast given us birth;
We give to Thee praises for Thy mercy towards us.

("Records of Past," ii, 133, quoted by Hoare in his "Religion of the Ancient Egyptians.") Now, this hymn, taken from the oldest monuments of the Egyptians, is no exception, found exclusively amongst them, and not to be found, at least in substance, in the teaching of other ancient peoples. Indeed, the more modern research and investigation have probed the religious history of the greatest peoples of antiquity, so much the more does the truth come out that all men in early times held firmly to a belief in one great Supreme Divinity. They may have raised up secondary powers to whom they paid worship or respect—the pure religion of Monotheism may by degrees have been obscured; but what appears to come out more and more clearly every day is this: that the highest and most cultured peoples of the most ancient times of all give witness to that *sensus numinis*, which led them spontaneously to worship the All-powerful and All-beneficent Creator of the Universe.

Having looked at the temper of the ancient Egyptians, now turn, for one instant, to another ancient and widespread people. What was the aboriginal religion in Hindostan? The myriads of that teeming country, though they possessed inferior gods and speak of oblations and sacrifices to them, still they made a vast distinction between these and the Almighty God of heaven and earth. This is evident to any one who studies the "Institutes of Menu." They say: "The triliteral monosyllable (om or aum) is an emblem of the Supreme; the suppressions of breath with a mind fixed on God are the highest devotion, but nothing is more exalted than the *gayatri*." "All rites ordained in the Veda, oblations of fire and solemn sacrifices, pass away; but that which passes not away is declared to be the syllable om, since it is a symbol of God, the Lord of created beings." "The act of repeating His holy name is ten times better than the appointed sacrifices." Again, "The four domestic sacraments, accompanied with the appointed sacrifice, are not equal all together to a sixteenth part of the act performed by a repetition of the *gayatri*." Now, my point will be brought out by explaining what this *gayatri* is. It is evidently far superior to invocations and adorations of the elements of Nature. What, then, is it? It is a solemn act of the worship of the Almighty God under the beautiful figure of the sun. Sir William Jones thus translates this act of adoration, which at once shows how vividly the minds of the millions of the Hindoo people, of that people in their aboriginal condition, were lighted up by that *sensus numinis* which illuminates every man who comes into this world, and compelled to offer the adoration of their hearts to the one great God of heaven and earth.

These are the words of the *gayatri:* "Let us adore the supremacy of that Divine Sun,"—*not the visible luminary, but*—"the Godhead who illuminates all, who recreates all, from whom all proceed, to whom all must return, whom we invoke to direct our understandings aright in our progress towards His holy seat." "This was the most sacred verse of the Vedas," says Father Thebaud, "whose recitation, according to the code of Menu, was not only far above all high expressions of awe in presence of the elements, but was to proceed all the religious acts of the Brahmins." "How could they," he asks, "have been at any time worshippers of the forces of Nature when anteriorly and at the same time they acknowledged such an infinitely Superior Being? It is repeatedly declared in the Menu code that all ceremonies and rites are nothing compared to the adoration of the SUPREME." ("Gentilism; Aboriginal Religion of Hindostan," p. 134-5.)

Listen to the teachings of this great people in their very earliest times, as translated from the Vedas by Sir William Jones: "What the sun and light are to this visible world, that is the Supreme Good and Truth to the intellectual and invisible universe; and as our corporeal eyes have a distinct perception of objects enlightened by the sun, thus our souls acquire sure knowledge by meditating on the light of truth which emanates from the Being of beings; *that* is the light by which alone our minds can be directed in the path of beatitude." "Without hand or foot He runs rapidly, and grasps firmly; without eyes He sees; without ears He hears *all;* He knows whatever can be known, but there is none who knows Him; Him the wise call the Great, Supreme, Pervading Spirit." And as our great theologians give us paraphrases on Scripture, so did the ancient Hindoo theologians write paraphrases on the Vedas. What could be more striking than the following description of the Almighty : " Perfect truth; perfect happiness; without equal ; immortal; absolute unity ; whom neither speech can describe, nor mind comprehend; all pervading; all transcending ; delighted with his own boundless intelligence ; not limited by space or time ; without feet, moving swiftly ; without hands, grasping all worlds ; without eyes, all-surveying; without ears, all-hearing ; without an exterior guide, understanding all; without cause, the first of all causes; all-ruling, all-powerful ; the creator, preserver, transformer of all things ; such is the Great One : this the Vedas declare." Now, turn for one moment to the present day. Compare the two theologies together, that which was written in the Hindostan some three thousand years ago and more, and that written in the nineteenth century in which we live. Shut the Vedas and its commentary and open the "Grammar of Assent," written by the great Oratorian theologian. How does he describe the Divine Being? In his section, headed "Belief in God," he writes thus : "There is one God, such and such in nature and attributes. I say 'such and such,' for unless I explain what I mean by 'one God,' I use words which may mean anything or nothing. I may mean a mere *anima mundi*, or an initial principle which once was in action and now is not, or collective humanity. I speak, then, of the God of the Theist and of the Christian : a God who is numerically One, who is Personal ; the Author, Sustainer and Finisher of all things, the Life of Law and Order, the Moral Governor; One who is Supreme and Sole; like Himself, unlike all things beside Himself, which all are but His creatures ; distinct from, independent of them all ; One who is self-existing, absolutely infinite, who has ever been and ever will be, to whom nothing is past or future, who is all perfection, and the fulness and archetype of every possible excellence, the Truth itself, Wisdom, Love, Justice, Holiness; One who is All-powerful, All-knowing, Omnipresent, Incomprehensible. These are some of the distinctive prerogatives which I ascribe unconditionally and unreservedly to the great Being whom I call God."

Now, how do you account for the very striking likeness between the picture of God painted by the Hindoo theologian some three thousand years ago, and that sketched by Dr. Newman in his study-room at Birmingham in the nineteenth century of the Christian era? Evidently, many and very contradictory pictures could be drawn; but how is it that the Catholic and Christian theologian harmonizes so strikingly with those great men of past ages who were the leaders and exponents of religious thought to myriads of their fellow-creatures in India and Egypt, and in the highest civilized countries of that ancient world that has passed away? It is because all the world over, where crime has not wholly obscured the light, the *sensus numinis* has been one and the same in all men. The nearer you approach to primitive times, the purer the knowledge and the worship. Being the self-same God, the nations of past days saw and acknowledged what we see and acknowledge; and the history in ancient times, the more it is studied, proves so much the more that the pressure of God's existence on the human mind is so weighty that, practically speaking, the whole world has been subdued by it, and takes it, indeed, as a first principle, for granted. What Chevalier says of Egypt, can, with equal truth, be predicated of all the oldest nations of the earth, in proportion to their culture and their gifts. He says: "The more we go up towards the origin of the Egyptian nation, the clearer we find, in their primitive purity, the principles of the natural law revealed to man at first by God Himself; the adoration of one only God, Creator of the world and of man; paternal authority, and the respect due to parents by their children; the love of one's neighbor; the necessity of labor; the immortality of the soul, and due rewards and punishments after this life. But the more we go down in time, the further from the cradle of primitive society, the more altered we find the primordial truths and divine traditions by the invasion of Polytheism, which had perverted everything on earth when the Redeemer finally appeared." (The *Correspondent*, August, 1872.)

I might easily bring before your notice examples of this same fact sufficient to prove that the whole human race declares, and has declared, with a persistence and a universality which may be called the common sense of mankind, that whilst men are separated by a wall of brass from the brute creation, they are, on the other hand, creatures made by an Omnipotent, All-wise, All-powerful and All-good Creator. With the earth and all animate things that creep or run upon it at his feet, man looks up to the heavens above him, and feels an intimate and sovereign conviction, which nothing but idiotcy or crime can rob him of, that he is a creature, and, therefore, has a Creator; that he is finite, and, therefore, there is an Infinite; that he hears the voice of conscience silently, yet forcibly, speaking to him and approving of good and condemning evil, and that, therefore, there is a Divine Law-giver and Master, who, having created him, wrote those laws in his heart, and becomes the Personal, ever-present Judge before whose tribunal he feels that he ever stands, and under whose All-seeing Eye and All-piercing intelligence he lives and moves and has his being. True, these dictates and convictions may, through training and education and pure life, be more vivid and intense in some than in others; wickedness may blot them out, but with all who exercise properly the faculties that God has given them, the light of the great truth of God's existence and personal love for man shines with brilliancy enough to subdue the mind; and when to this light are added the multitudinous and converging arguments and indications *ab extra* of the truth of this primary fact; then man is bound intellectually and morally, unless he would trample on the being God has given him, unless he would deny reason itself, to submit and declare, in the words of Dr. Newman, who is looked on as one of the most cautious of modern thinkers, that the only two absolute luminously self-evident beings are himself and his Creator; or if you prefer the words of the sceptic, David Hume, the fact of the existence of God is an unquestionable and self-evident truth; that is to say, in other words, Hume and Newman agree in this, that to deny the existence of God would be equivalent to denying that two and two are four, or that the three angles of a triangle are equal to two right angles. These are necessary truths; they *must* be so; they cannot be otherwise; directly the mind of man is capable of grasping the meaning of the terms, he at once is compelled to give absolute interior assent to their truth; whilst to deny them, even according to Hume, would be to acknowledge himself to be crazy, or a man who is telling a conscious and deliberate untruth, or one who will not study the matter in hand.

Permit me to enlarge on this most important subject a little further. Allow me to bring before your attention the explanation of the fact why some people do not appear to be able to bring absolute syllogistic proof of the existence of God forward, such as would wholly satisfy their minds, on paper. This being the case does not even tend to militate against the truth or the luminousness of the truth of God's existence. Indeed, it is to be expected that such a momentous and wide-reaching truth as this cannot be shoved for its proof into a nutshell. The syllogism can do many things; and perhaps a million syllogisms converging from different quarters, if the force of that million syllogisms could be gathered together in one focus, like the rays of the sun, by means of a burning-glass, might so affect the reason as to compel it at once and absolutely to submit. But this cannot be done; we reason from point to point; we have to leave one thing to get hold of another. Whilst I am proving God's existence from creation, I am blank regarding His voice in the conscience; when I am proving Him from the doctrine of causes, I have already placed on one side the proofs from the moral sense; whilst I am engaged in showing the power of the *sensus numinis*, I have discharged the arguments drawn from the common agreement of mankind; my logical forces are scattered; and I find the processes of paper logic inadequate to so great an argument, and incapable of bringing to bear upon my whole being as a man, and at one stamp, the whole united pressure of that one overwhelming argument which is made up of ten thousand subtle influences, which affect not solely my logic-chopping and conclusion-drawing faculty, but my spiritual nature, down to its deepest and inmost depths; my heart, with all its vast capacities for love; and my very senses themselves, that are not made of stone, and that respond through every fibre of my body to this pressure on my intellectual and moral being and on my conscience, in one word, on my entire man. Who can analyze or convey in words the influence and fascination for the soul of a passionate burst of music? Who could in rough material words describe and convey those inexplicable impressions of the sublime in nature and art which from time to time affect us? or explain syllogistically the force and intensity of that absorbing, self-immolating passion which we call a mother's love? Who could analyze and bring out as a conclusion of logic the conviction in the mind which is hinted at by the poet when he speaks of those whom we love and are dead, yet still live and think of us, and whom we *know* do live? Why do we know that the poet is speaking our mind as well as his own, when he exclaims:

> Oh, hearts that never cease to yearn!
> Oh, brimming tears that ne'er are dried!
> The dead, though they depart, return,
> As if they had not died!
>
> The living are they only dead;
> The dead live—never more to die;
> And often when we mourn them fled,
> They never were so nigh!

Here syllogisms are of no avail. They are altogether out of court, and have to be banished as useless and impertinent intruders. They cannot furnish us with one half of the deepest proofs we possess of God's existence; and to imagine that they are capable of furnishing us with all is to say that love can be analyzed, that conscience can be cut into major, minor, and conclusion, and that those profound emotions which spring from the heart can form the conclusions of *Barbar* or *Celarent*. The *sensus numinis*, the moral sense, the gift of intellectual insight and perception precede all reasoning, and form a class of motives which impress upon us with their sovereign luminous force the primary fact of the existence of a Personal God. What the scientific man takes for granted, and is obliged to take for granted, before he starts in quest of truth from Nature, does not possess half the brilliancy and light that this truth of God's existence possesses, and which even if Nature outside of us were silent, we should be able reasonably to hold, on account of the testimonies of the *sensus numinis* alone. But this apart; it is thus that proof on paper, or paper logic, is unsatisfactory. A thing cannot do satisfactorily what it was never made to do at all. We look at our syllogism, and feel convinced that there is some other influence on us beside that dry major, minor, and conclusion; and we are puzzled how it happens that we are so absolutely convinced, and yet that we should find so great a difficulty in reducing our motives for being so to paper.

If you will allow me, I will suggest one method which I can recommend to you as facilitating the entrance of proof or light from various quarters into the mind. I will explain myself by an example. Let me take a necessary truth, that shines with its own light, and which you are bound to admit the truth of, if you claim to remain rational creatures. It is this: "Every trilinear figure is triangular." Perhaps there are not many people here who do not happen to have studied geometry who are cognizant of this fact. To know it, therefore, it must be pondered on; and the more you ponder on it, so much the more absolutely convinced are you that it is self-evidently and luminously true. Moreover, when once you have imagined one trilinear figure, and examined to see if it be really triangular, you will at once, simply by having examined this one, declare that all other imaginary trilinear figures must be triangular also; to deny this, you feel, would be to deny the soundness of your faculties, and to declare yourself incapable of tought. Now take the three letters

G—O—D. At first sight they are but three letters of our alphabet, and nothing else. But ponder on them. Fill up the full meaning of them; and, in proportion as you understand them, will the truth of that Being's existence which they represent impress itself upon your mind as being a necessary truth, as impressive, as sovereign in its claim upon your adhesion, as the truth that every figure with three lines must have three angles. If some find it at once difficult to realize this, the fault is in themselves, and not in the light offered them.

If you draw down the blinds or shut the shutters of your room, the sun may be pouring down in his noon-day flood, and you will remain in utter darkness; but throw open the shutters, pull up the blinds, open the windows, and let in the full stream of light "from all parts of the hemisphere of heaven," and your eyes will then acknowledge the existence of that great luminary which, though obscured by cloud or fog, in the order of Nature, occupies an analogous position to the Divine Illuminator, whose existence is proclaimed by ten thousand converging lights from without, as well as by the light He Himself creates in the conscience and intelligence of man. I say, then, that when a man, as a man, has taken those three letters G—O—D, and has filled up their meaning, so far as is in him, from the cumulus of arguments which, when thrown into one, form the grand overwhelming proof for God's existence; when he has done that, and has allowed the force of evidence, united and drawn together into one focus, so as to make one single stamp or seal upon man's entire being, to fix itself on his soul; when that has fairly been done, then man is as much bound to submit, or, rather, to rise up, to the acknowledgement of the great truth of God's existence, personal love and watchful providence, as he is bound to admit, if he would not declare himself bereft of reason, that every trilateral figure in geometry is a triangular one. In one word, to draw a conclusion from Hume's premises, unless we declare ourselves idiots, or conscious liars, or drugged by vice, or self-deceived by pride or passion, or careless of argument, we are compelled, through a double pressure, that of objective truth without, and of subjective certainty within, to join in the *consensus* of human kind in all ages and every zone, and declare that God exists, the Creator and Ruler of the world. Does not Pope, one of our greatest Catholic poets, express in verse this ubiquitous and profound conviction when he puts the following prayer in the mouth of universal humanity, exclaiming with equal depth and simplicity:

> Father of all! in every age,
>   In every clime adored,
> By saint, by savage, and by sage,
>   Jehovah, Jove or lord!
>
> The great First Cause, least understood,
>   Who all my sense confined
> To know but this, that Thou art good,
>   And that myself am blind.
>
> *   *   *   *   *   *
>
> To Thee, whose temple is all space,
>   Whose altar, earth, sea, skies!
> One chorus let all beings raise!
> All Nature's incense rise!

In conclusion, then, I venture to express a hope that men of good will are satisfied that I have adduced sufficient cause for their holding as a reasonable doctrine that He does really exist who thus appeals to the entire man— appeals through the myriad converging rays of light striking into the soul from without, and through that fountain of life within, in the conscience, which, whilst it reflects those rays, shoots up, as it were, into the heavens, and spontaneously declares, as a relief to the pent-up energies of the spirit, that "the Lord, He is God; He made us, and not we ourselves!"

Next Sunday evening, I shall employ myself in showing you what misery and degradation man, and what chaos society would be reduced to, if the theory of the Religion of Denial were treated as a fact; if man were simply a mud-fish, which had achieved a certain number of improvements; and if the idea of God's existence were merely a stupid blunder swimming on the brain of such a mud-fish. Destroy man, and you cannot prove God; destroy God, and there is nothing but degradation, despair and death for man.

DENIAL.

The fourth lecture of Archbishop Vaughan's series on the reasonableness of Christianity and the shallowness of unbelief was delivered by His Grace at St. Mary's, Sydney, Australia, on Sunday evening, March 30, and, despite the threatening aspect of the weather, the church was packed. The subject of the discourse was "Denial." His Grace said :—

During the last two Sunday evenings we have been engaged in establishing two all-important and primary truths—first, that man is not a brute, but that, on the contrary, he is endowed with gifts which separate him radically from irrational beings; and secondly, that there is a God, who is our Lord, Master and Creator, the Rewarder of those who serve Him. We have, moreover, taken into our consideration the especial characteristics of man's nature, which make him spontaneously tend towards a Being better, purer, more powerful than himself; and we have seen, by the way in which God condescends to man, as well as by the way that man yearns and struggles up to God, that there is a reciprocal action and-re-action, man knowing his God through the light of reason, and loving Him with the power of his will; and God, in return, uniting Himself to man, and becoming his reward exceeding great, not merely in a future state, but in the present condition of his existence, and through all the obscurities which envelop the actualities of life. Thus we have established the most important starting-points from which to argue, upon which to build that fabric of religion which not only addresses itself to the conscience, but also, by its reasonableness, solicits the assent of all serious men who are seeking for truth in order that, when they have found it, they may embrace it.

And as the fabric of religion can be raised upon the foundations of those great facts,—of man being what I have shown him to be, and of the existence of God,—as these are the two necessary corner-stones of the spiritual edifice; so it follows that, if these two corner-stones be removed, that edifice which they supported will inevitably come to the ground. The denial, in one word, of man's manhood and of God's existence—the latter denial necessarily following from the former—is the absolute death-blow of all religion, morality and philosophy worthy of the name.

It will be, then, my task this evening to unveil before you the character of, and the consequences which flow from the religion of Denial; and to show you that it represents a method of teaching and a school of thought which are calculated to destroy and corrupt whatever is beautiful in humanity, and noble and pure in the aspirations of the heart. It will be my place to point out to you its unfitness as a substitute for even the lowest forms of Christianity; and to draw your attention to the fact that, principally through the ignorance of the multitude, it is making, and has made, in the past few years a large number of converts to its teachings; and is likely, unless those who can speak do speak, and speak boldly and logically, too, to make great havoc amidst the rising generation, who, having little leisure for the exercise of deep philosophical speculation, are led away with facility by such as push themselves forward as oracles of Science and as leaders in the van of "modern thought." It will be my duty to point out to you, and to give you my reasons for saying so, that no curse could be imagined greater than for this black death to visit your homes, and to get into and eat away the hearts and intellects of your children, robbing them, as it would inevitably do, of all that makes life bearable, of all that gives it meaning, and of that which offers to its deepest griefs and sorest trials an unguent which does away with more than half their sting. I shall give you cause for feeling that it is your duty, your solemn obligation, to resist to the uttermost the approaches of this blighting and death-breathing plague; and to make yourselves apostles of the Christian creed by possessing yourselves of the arguments which support it, and by displaying the miserable drivel of that pretended form of science which loves to root up and to destroy, but is absolutely incapable of creating a coherent creed, an intelligible or tenable philosophy, a morality worthy of any reasonable being possessing the initial notions of right and wrong, or any form of consistent thought fitted to the essential wants of the human spirit.

It is my purpose to give sufficient cause for all reasonable men to come to the conclusion that the Religion of Denial is a shallow religion; that it promises very great things, greater than ever have been attained by man, and egregiously fails to carry out that promise; that, in point of fact, it not merely is an imposture, but one of the most mischievous and damning impostures that have ever been started by cultured men, and that, were it once to take root, and enter into the substance of human thought on a large scale, it would produce the most frightful anarchy, and end by tearing up the whole social order, not to speak of the religious and moral, root and branch. Having done this, I shall proceed to show you how such a state of things as this, when brought to bear upon the point of these lectures, is a strong argument in favor of convincing honest men of the reasonableness of Christianity; for, if a religion excogitated by the ablest and most scientific of modern minds, by men who have earned for themselves the name of "advanced thinkers," is found to be, when brought to the test, absolutely unfitted to be a religion at all; if the best modern attempt, in comparison with Christianity, is proved to be simply a ridiculous and impracticable dream, and a very bad dream, too; then surely it is but reasonable and prudent to fall back upon that system which it has proved itself unable to supplant; and to come to the conclusion that Christianity, after all, after so many efforts have been made to invent something better than it—and those efforts have absolutely failed—is the best form of religion which a sane and serious man, under existing circumstances, could adopt. True, the fact of Denial being false does not prove Christianity true; but the fact of Christianity doing what Denial promises to do, and never succeeds in doing, is a witness, as far as it goes, in favor of Christianity; and when the fact is remembered of my having proved already the falsity of the Negative basis, and the truth of the Christian one— the spirituality of man and the existence of a God from whom Nature and Grace proceed—the fact of my having uprooted the corner-stones of the Religion of Denial, and of having shown how those of Christianity cling, as it were, to the living rock of fundamental truth; this fact, I say, when coupled with the utter failure of the Religion of Denial, and comparative success of Christianity as a working system, would induce any reasonable man to reject absolutely, and without compromise, the former, and give his earnest and sincere adhesion to the latter. Thus the reasoning I urge against the shallow pretensions of Denial turn into an Argument for the reasonableness of Christianity. And it is the task of developing this thought that I have imposed on myself this evening.

Now, what is the position of that school of modern thought representing the Religion of Denial? Its position is the result of two, or rather, of one main assumption, which it starts with as an absolute and dogmatic fact, namely, that man, and all he is and does, body, soul and senses, is evolved and devolved from a piece of carbon, combined with sulphur and some few other ingredients. He is essentially and exclusively of the earth, earthy. Certainly, as the seed grows, as a grain of corn sprouts, thrusts its tender leaves through the rough earth, expands them, and develops into leaf and ear, and ripens into the blade, so does man grow and spread out from the protoplasm, or, if you will, the mud-fish, into his present development and flower. To some person this might seem a theory as harmless as it appears to them ridiculous. And such might have been the case had it been started by low and ignorant fanatics, without name or position in the learned or scientific world. But this theory springs from those sublime heights, the Olympus, where dwell the "advanced thinkers" of the age, and, as all those who have not time or skill to verify data for themselves, and who compose the vast majority of mankind, have to take their "science" on authority, just as the generality of men have to take their religion on authority, it follows that, if scientific men teach falsehoods, and assert as a dogma what is merely a clumsy hypothesis, the masses of the people will be led astray by them, and, what is worse, will begin, and do begin, to call in question those fundamental positions on which all happiness and virtue rest, and to lose perhaps forever that faith, and hope and love which are the great solace of suffering, toiling humanity in this world below.

And this has actually been the case. Those votaries of Natural Science who are the enemies of Revelation and the opponents of Religion, have already succeeded in infusing into general society a spirit of scepticism, irreverance and recklessness, which are harbingers of grave perils for the future. Having done their best to bring Religion into disrepute with the masses of the people, these modern lights set about building, amidst the ruins of what they have destroyed, their own especial Temple to the Unknown or the Unthinkable; a Temple and a religious system far more brutalizing than the basest theogonies and the most grovelling mythologies of the ancients. Let it be remembered that principles are inexorable, that logic is merciless, and that man naturally, in course of time, will drive the principles given him to their logical conclusions. The wedge will be sent home. The world of action is governed and swayed by the world of thought; and the restless mind of the masses of the people, helped on by fairly educated, but unscientific thinkers, is excessively quick in applying to the actualities of life those fundamental principles which, when looked at in themselves, seem as if they had issued from the brain of a recluse, and would never be likely to go much further than the cloister.

The cardinal principle of the Religion of Denial represents one of these fundamental principles. It was born in the brain of a student; and has, like those dark, harmless-looking grains of blast powder which are able to shiver the hardest rock, in appearance nothing dangerous-looking about it; but, in spite of that, it is charged with a power of moral and spiritual destruction capable of smashing and scattering abroad the traditions of ages and the teachings of the most venerable philosophy. Grant that man sprang from the mud-fish, and you have upset Christianity, and left the world a black ruin in a howling wilderness.

And how is this so? Because water will not rise above its source. Because, as the axiom has it, *Nemo dat quod non habet;* because, in a word, a mud-fish will be only a mud-fish, and all the development in the world, and all the evolutions imaginable, and the influence of the most favorable environment, even were it possible, of the cherubim and seraphim themselves, would never make anything more out of a mud-fish than a dab of protoplastic mud. Thus, as logic says, that the conclusion of a syllogism has no more strength than the weakest link in the chain of reasoning, so here, the highest and noblest aspiration of the mud-fish will simply be the vomiting forth of its own mud, and will have nothing whatever to do with anything purer, cleaner or more transparent than itself. It is easy to see what havoc such a principle as this would make amongst all those teachings of Christianity, of Natural and Supernatural Religion, of morality and philosophy, which are prized so highly by civilized mankind. It is easy to see, if this assumption be admitted as a victorious discovery of Science, that man *ipso facto* ceases to be man; that his highest ideals are merely so much sublimated mud; that his deepest convictions regarding the existence of God, of virtue, of morality, of freedom—that all his cherished and most ennobling maxims of life and of sacrifice, when thrown fairly in the balance, cannot weigh more than himself—when tested and analyzed cannot, by any possibility, be found worth more than the mud under one's feet, than the scream of a frightened monkey, or the dreams of a sleeping owl. Thus, all is brought down to one dead and fetid level. Man ceases to be man; his freedom is gone, for he acts through the force of necessity; and all his high imaginings are but the gilding of a summer cloud, more deceptive, and equally unsubstantial. Thus, self-sacrifice loses all its meaning; the devotedness of pure women and the courage of brave men lose all their charm; the generosity, nobility, and elevation of spirit, which have ever been admired as the outcome of chosen natures, are neither better nor worse than debauchery, brutality and crime, and the very temples of Religion itself—those vast spiritual creations which have been built up by theologians, and are as suggestive as epic poems of the greatness and the love of the Supreme, fade into unmeaningness. The intellect and imagination become emptied of any valuable spiritual or moral furniture; and, if this assumption were once admitted as a fact by the masses of mankind, if it were once established, as Christianity now is, as the creed of the greatest and foremost civilized community on earth, then we might apply to the order of thought what the poet says of the materia order when he tells us that—

> The cloud-capp'd tower, the gorgeous palaces,
> The solemn temples, the great globe itself,
> Yea, all which it inherit, shall dissolve;
> And, like this unsubstantial pageant, faded,
> Leave not a rock behind.

Of course, our leading scientific men, through habit and education, are cautious in their utterances, and guarded almost up to the point of cowardice, in declaring to the world their distinct convictions. Still the world is very sharp. To throw doubt on the existence of God, to speak in vague terms of it, to seem afraid of being committed to a bold declaration of it, to define His nature and attributes in almost unintelligible terms, all these practices tend directly to create suspicion in the public mind, and prepare the way for bolder speakers, if not more reckless thinkers, to drive the wedge of Denial still further home. Take, for instance, Mr. Tyndal, who has gained the ear of the British public. Why cannot he speak out? Why, in a vital question of life or death, speak in poetry or in enigma? Listen to the following, and you will at once apprehend my meaning:—

"Whence come we; whither go we? The question dies without an answer—*without even an echo*—upon the infinite shores of the Unknown. Let us follow matter to its utmost bounds; let us claim it in all its forms to experiment with and to speculate upon. Casting the term 'vital force' from our vocabulary, let us reduce, if we can, the visible phenomena of life to mechanical attractions and repulsions. Having thus exhausted physics and reached its very rim, the real mystery still looms beyond us. We have, in fact, made no step towards its solution. And thus it will ever loom, even beyond the bourne of knowledge, compelling the philosophies of successive ages to confess that

'We are such stuff
As dreams are made of, and our little life
Is rounded with a sleep.'"

("Use and Limit of the Imagination of Science.")

Now, how can Mr. Tyndal say that the question dies "without even an echo?" Is not this making use of Science to generate doubt? Does he mean that neither philosophy nor logic, when brought to bear on the data he provides for us, can, with all their questionings, elicit the echo of an answer? Does he mean to give a flat contradiction to the united voice of all, or nearly all, great men on this momentous question? If he does, he should distinctly say so; if he does not, why not tell us? Why leave the world under the impression that man is blind and plunged in everlasting darkness, and that it is best for him to look on his existence as an empty dream?

Again, when this same popular professor was censured for his Belfast Address, he published the following apology, which shows how enigmatical are the utterances of these first-class scientific men upon matters of the most momentous import which they will not boldly deal with, and yet will not leave alone. "In a recent speech at Dewsbury," he says, "the Dean of Manchester is reported to have expressed himself thus: 'The Professor [myself] ended a most remarkable and eloquent speech by terming himself a material Atheist.' For myself, I use no language which could imply that I am hurt by such attacks. They have lost their power to wound or injure. So, likewise, as regards a resolution recently passed by the Presbytery of Belfast, in which Professor Huxley and myself are spoken of as 'ignoring the existence of God, and advocating pure and simple Materialism.' Had the possessive pronoun 'our' preceded 'God,' and had the words 'what we consider' preceded 'pure,' this statement would have been objectively true; but to make it so, this qualification is required." It is strange to unsophisticated thinkers that these men, who are so severe in admitting anything they cannot understand, should invent propositions that few can imagine the meaning of, except, perhaps, themselves; or should fashion to themselves such a God as cannot be made fairly intelligible to an ordinary intelligence. Anyhow, such cowardly philosophy tends to bring the idea of the Supreme Being gradually into contempt. And yet, it is listened to and produces its effect. Men of science have gained the public ear, and deservedly so, in many ways;

but all men of science are not scientific men; some of them are athletes of infidelity, and make use of the authority which science has acquired for fixing in the mind of second-class thinkers and the public principles which may look very harmless, but which carry within them a species of spiritual blast-powder which produces destruction wherever it is scattered. So is it with the Religion of Denial, which is based upon the principle of the protoplasm or the mud-fish, and which begins and ends with that from which it springs. As I remarked, scientific men of the first-class, who are bent upon pushing their Religion of Denial upon the world, do so with a certain prudence, and with caution. They feel that the world is not yet prepared for a flat denial of God, the spirituality of the soul, and a future state; they, therefore, preach a vague and careful doctrine; praising "Science" as the only logical and intellectual method of discovering Truth; declaring Religion to be a mere "Faith," which has worn itself out, and that did very well before the science of verification had been duly understood, but which now is fit only for priests who live by it, for old women who live upon the priests, and for the masses of the people who are too ignorant to be taught. Having thus placed "Science" on a pedestal on account of its supposed superior method, and cast Religion to the earth, because it is alleged by them to be worn out, these men proceed to teach the world that though they do not deny the existence of God, they cannot affirm His existence; and that He is in fact unknowable; and that mysteries are not for them; and that man had better not entangle himself with questions he cannot possibly solve; that "Science" merely tells us phenomena, and that essences are beyond all ken; and that, therefore, the world must do its best, and worship itself if it must worship something, as, in reality, there is nothing else for it to worship; for who could bend the knee to an abstraction, or offer sacrifice to the unknowable and unthinkable, and love and adore one knows not what, that inhabits one knows not where? This is the position which our foremost thinkers of the Religion of Denial occupy in England; this is the teaching of Tyndal, Huxley and Herbert Spencer, men who have exerted, and still do exert, on account of their name as scientific men, and because of their brilliant literary style, an influence over the mind of England that can scarcely be exaggerated. What these men have started has been carried out boldly by less cautious writers than themselves; and the doubt or uncertainty, or, at all events, the unsatisfactory position which they are satisfied to give to primary religious truths, has been used with advantage by men more eager even than themselves to defy Scienc, or, at least, to melt Religion out of the minds of their fellow-men.

Take, for instance, the teaching of two leading German philosophers and two leading Englishmen regarding the nature of Almighty God, and you will see at once how their theories lead directly towards suspicion and distrust. Having dismissed the God of Christianity, Strauss at once substitutes his own. "We believe in no God," says he, "but only in self-poised and amidst eternal changes constant universum." Hartmann says: "God is a personification of force." Our own Mill says God is "a being of great but limited power, how or by what limited we cannot even conjecture." Matthew Arnold teaches that God is "a power, not ourselves, that makes for righteousness." William Marr sweeps away all gods as so many cobwebs, and says: "Faith in a personal and living God is the origin and fundamental cause of our miserable social condition. . . . The true road to liberty, to equality, and to happiness is Atheism. No safety on earth so long as man holds on by a thread to heaven. Let nothing henceforth shackle the spontaneity of the human kind. Let us teach man that there is no other God than *himself;* that he is the Alpha and Omega of all things, the superior being, and the most real reality." From this blasphemous declaration, which is the basis of the Religion of Denial, follows a host of tenets which lead to man's moral and spiritual corruption, and which are popularized by thinkers of a second class amongst the masses.

Professor Norre, in Germany, has contributed his share to the popular literature. Here are one or two specimens of his philosophy: "Man possesses many internal qualities, such as imagination and the milt." "An external quality is seeing, an internal one is digestion." "Thought is a secretion of the brain, and other secretions come from the kidneys." "Man is what he eats." That such views as these have permeated amongst the masses of the people in Germany, and have become popular even with ladies of high cultivation, is evident from the writings of many amongst them. For example, a lady-disciple of Prof. Moleschott publishes a series of letters, in which as a specimen of the rest, I select the following passage: "The moral rule for each man is given by his own nature only, and is different, therefore, for each individual. What are excesses and passions by themselves? Nothing but a larger or smaller overflowing of a perfectly legitimate impulse." Take one more example, which carries the principle still further, from the writings of another lady-philosopher. She exclaims: "Enjoyment is good, and frenzy and love are good, but hatred also. Hatred answers well when we cannot have love. Wealth is good, because it can be changed into enjoyment. Power is good, because it satisfies our pride. Truth is good, so long as it gives us pleasure, but good is lying, also, and perjury, hypocrisy, trickery, flattery, if they secure us any advantage. Faithfulness is good, so long as it pays, but treason is good also, if it fetches a higher price. Marriage is good, so long as it makes us happy; but good is adultery, also, for every one who is tired of marriage, or who happens to fall in love with a married person. Fraud is good, theft, robbery and murder, if they lead to wealth and enjoyment. Life is good, so long as it is a riddle; good is suicide, also, after the riddle has been guessed. But as every enjoyment culminates in our being deceived and tired and as the last pleasure vanishes with the last illusion, he only would seem to be truly wise who draws the last conclusion of all science, *i. e.*, who takes prussic acid, and that without delay." (See Max Muller's "Origin of Reason," p. 478.)

Take some of the popular teachings in modern philosophy, and you will see at a glance how they lead to the above doctrines of moral anarchy and spiritual death:—

"There is nothing real but body." God and the soul are "methaphysical entities, bubbles of soap." We may well be the fruit of successive modifications, wrought upon ancestors far less perfect than we are, and even next in order to great apes." Investigations are *en chasse* "to find" the man-ape, the animal which according to them must have been the transition between apes and man. "God, banished from Science, took refuge in Metaphysics. . . The idea of God is already well shaken. We must still give it the last blow." "The name soul must be reserved for the assemblage of faculties of the central nervous system taken as a whole." "Thought is inherent in the substance of the brain only as it is nourished, like the contractile power of the muscles." "An idea is the product of a combination analogous to formic acid; thought depends on phosphorous contained in the substance of the brain; virtue, devotedness, and courage are organic currents of electricity." "Virtue and vice are products, like sugar and vitriol." Professor Moleschott writes and teaches thus: "The will is the necessary expression of a state of the brain produced by external influences. There is no such thing as free will. A crime is the logical result, direct and inevitable, of the passion which animates us. Without phosphorous, no thought. *Sans phosphore point de pensee.* . . "Thought is a movement of matter, conscience is also a property of matter." The path is easy, from such doctrines as these, to the assertion that man is a brute. "What essential difference is there between man and the dog, and why should we hesitate to do to the one what we do daily to the other?" is a question based upon these principles. Jubal, in Dr. Newman's "Callista," expresses the same conclusion as the result of his pagan principles. "Our first duty is to seek our own happiness," he exclaims, "if a man thinks it happier to be a hog, why let him be a hog." ("Callista," p. 34.) It is strange how inevitably these principles of Denial, when once started or made starting points, lead directly toward dragging man down to the brute creation. When once a man has lost his hold on God and his own conscience, he seems compelled, as it were, to deny his own manhood, and to sink at once into the "sensual mire" of his lower, coarser nature.

To illustrate this by one or two more examples. For instance, Dr. Lewins boldly teaches: "Earth *is* Paradise if the healthy operation of every anatomical structure could be preserved. . . . . . . All that is fabled by poets, saints, martyrs, founders of sects and systems, under the term Saturnian, or Golden Age, Kingdom of Heaven, Paradise, etc., is comprehended in that supreme *bien etre* which results from the equilibrium of the bodily functions." ("Life and Mind.") Professor Hartmann, to whom I referred in my Introductory Address, teaches as follows: "It is important to make the beast life better known to youth as being the truest source of pure nature, wherein they may learn to understand *their true being* in its simplest form, and in it rest and refresh themselves after the artificiality and deformity of our social condition. . . . Let us only think how *agreeably* an *ox* or a *hog* lives, almost as if he had learned to do so from Aristotle." ("Philosophie des Unbewusten," p. 359.) It would almost seem that I have now said enough to show you how the principle on which the Religion of Denial is based drags everything down to mere brutality. But it would be as well to allow Thomas Carlyle to throw into his own graphic form the results, as seen by him, of such principles in England. He seems to find men already much brutalized by the theories of the leading few, which the masses at once set about putting into practice, if they satisfy that greed and passion which lurks in the nature of all mankind.

He says: "The universe, so far as sane conjecture can go, is an immeasurable Swine's-trough, consisting of solid and liquid, and of other contrasts and kinds, especially consisting of attainable and unattainable, the latter in immensely greater quantities for some Pigs. Moral evil is unattainability of Pig's-wash; moral good attainability of ditto. What is Paradise or the state of innocence? Paradise, called state of innocence, age of gold, and other names, *was* (according to Pigs of weak judgment) unlimited attainability of Pig's-wash; perfect fulfillment of one's wishes, so that the Pig's imagination could not out-run reality; a fable and an impossibility, as Pigs of sense now see! Define the whole duty of Pigs. It is the mission of universal Pighood, and the duty of all Pigs, at all times, to diminish the quantity of unattainable and increase that of attainable. All knowledge and device and effort ought to be directed thither and thither only; Pig science, Pig enthusiasm and devotion has this one aim. It is the whole duty of Pigs. Pig poetry ought to consist of universal recognition of the excellence of Pig's-wash and ground barley, and the felicity of Pigs whose trough is in order, and who have had enough. Hrumph! who made the Pig? Unknown; perhaps the 'pork butcher.'" Now, all this, though a very gross way of putting things, simply throws into telling shape, and brings out, without any varnish on it, the practical outcome of the Religion of Denial; men are reduced to the dead-level of their supposed origin, and the strongest propension in them rules, as in other brutes, as a tyrannical despot over the rest. Carlyle also pictures very graphically the effects of such principles on the relations of man to man in daily life, and on the frame of mind which is encouraged by the Religion of Denial. He asks: "Have you law and justice in Pigdom? Pigs of observation have discerned that there is, or was once supposed to be, a thing called justice. Undeniably, at least, there is a sentiment in Pig-nature called indignation, revenge, &c., which, if one Pig provoke another, comes out in a more or less destructive manner; hence, laws are necessary, amazing quantities of laws. For quarrelling is attended with loss of blood, of life, at any rate, with frightful effusion of the general stock of Hog's-wash, and ruin (temporary ruin) to large sections of the universal Swine's-trough; wherefore let justice be observed, so that quarreling be avoided.

What is justice? Your own share of the general Swine's-trough, not any portion of my share. But what is 'my' share? Ah! there in fact lies the grand difficulty; upon which Pig-science, meditating this long while, can settle absolutely nothing. My share—hrumph!—my share is, on the whole, whatever I can contrive to get without being hanged or sent to the hulks."

Now turn to statistics, and see if Carlyle is very far out. Take authentic record of the condition of England at the present hour. I cut this passage as it stands out of a newspaper, reporting a speech of the Bishop of Salford: "During the five years ending 1824 there were 65,000 cases of crime recorded, but during a like period ending 1874 there were no less than 408,000 of such cases, or, in other words, crime had increased sixfold during the last half century, while the population had but doubled. Taking more recent dates, say from 1860 to 1874, assault had increased 36 per cent., breaches of peace 128 per cent., damage to property 69 per cent., misdemeanor 37 per cent., desertion of families 75 per cent., larceny 64 per cent., prostitution 36 per cent., people having no visible means of subsistance 73 per cent., drunkenness 110 per cent.,—more than double during the last fourteen years,—and all this while the population has only increased 18 per cent." So far what Carlyle says about "justice" being "whatever a man can contrive to get" is proved even more accurate than his own description. What do statistics tell us about Carlyle's "Pig's-trough?" They tell us that, last year, one hundred and fifty million pounds sterling were spent upon drink in England. The whole nation, last year, spent sixty millions in corn, and, of that quantity, eighty million bushels were thrown into the "Pig's-trough" in the shape of liquid alone—of drink. During the next five years, the "trough had to be enlarged because seven hundred and thirteen million pounds sterling were spent in filling it with liquor. That is to say, whilst the population had only increased 16 per cent., the drink had increased at the rate of 50 per cent.

Now turn for one moment to another subject. Whilst this debasing and brutalizing process has been going on at home, have the people been increasing in Christianity? Are they tending towards the Religion of Denial or towards that Religion which it so violently opposes? Have men been more and more impressed that they have "to be perfect as their Heavenly Father is Perfect," which is the Christian principle of morality and happiness; or that they have to enjoy themselves as hogs, if that happens to please them most, which is the fundamental principle of the Religion of Denial? Let me quote an enemy to Christianity on this point, and then a friend; and you will see how they bear the same testimony: "A very large proportion," says Greg, "probably the majority, of the operative class in towns, are total unbelievers; and these are not the reckless and disreputable, but, on the contrary, consist of the best of the skilled workmen, the most instructed and thoughtful, as well as the steadiest. The hard-headed, industrious reading engineers and foremen, the members of mechanics' institutes, the natural leaders of the artisans, are sceptics intellectually, not morally; they disbelieve because they have inquired, argued and observed, and have been unable to obtain from their Methodist fellow-workmen, or even from ministers of the Gospel, satisfactory answers to their doubts. Among manufacturing artisans and the highest description of citizen laborer, it may be stated with even more confidence than of the ranks above them in the social scale that the intellect of this body is already divorced from

the prevalent creeds of the country. The range and form
of this scepticism varies widely in the different classes.
Among workingmen it is for the most part absolute Atheism, and is complicated by a marked feeling of antagonism
towards the teachers of Religion, a kind of resentment
growing out of the conviction that they have been systematically deluded by those who ought to have enlightened
them. Thinkers of the higher order among the educated
classes, and more especially scientific men, by no means as
a rule go so far as this, but content themselves with pronouncing God to be unknowable and His existence unprovable; the distinctive doctrines of Christianity, and the
details of its historical basis neither made out nor in any
way admissable, and a future life to be a matter of pure
speculation, which may or may not be in store for us, but
as to which no rational man would dare to dogmatize.
Literary men and scholars are often sceptical merely as to
special creeds, though sincerely and deeply religious in tone
and temperament. But all concur in repudiating existing
forms of Christianity, that is, the common religion of the
nation; the Jehovah of the Bible, the heaven and hell of
divines and priests, the Resurrection of the Gospels and the
salvation, formulas of creeds and churches." (Greg's
"Rocks Ahead," p. 131) . . . . "The shrewd,
honest mechanic cannot half say one thing and half believe
another, and has no great respect or trust for the man who
can. His instrument of thought is not delicate enough to
play with dogmas, and want of downright assertion or
negation appears like want of integrity to him. He cannot
suspend his judgment; with him unbelief immediately and
inevitably becomes disbelief, and disbelief fast becomes
mixed with contempt and indignation towards the sceptic or
the half-believer, whom he regards as coquetting and tam-

pering with the unclean thing. Nebulus tenets, vague dissent, luminous conceptions, with a colored halo round them, are not for the skilled workman; he is angry with the teachers of a Church that has so long misled him, and seems bent on mystifying him still. When the lower classes reach the point, therefore, of abandoning Christianity, their rejection of it will be not, as often among the upper ranks, languid and reserved, but absolute, and, most probably, resentful. Their disbelief will be apt to be as intolerant and dogmatic as the credence of the orthodox." (Ibid, p. 138.)

Now take the words of a friend. "The advance of infidelity," says an able writer in *The Month*, "among a large portion of the generation now entering, or having entered, upon the full enjoyment and use of life, has reached the line, at which even morality becomes a sentiment rather than a law; conscience a phenomenon, rather than the voice of God sitting in judgment; free-will and responsibility an imagination; the universe a physical system, self-evolved and self-regulated; the soul of a man a mechanism; the future of a man a blank; sin, original and actual, a fiction; the Atonement, an impossible superstition." Again: "The advance of infidelity and of its inseparable shadow, immorality, among the lower classes in our towns, the extreme activity with which the poison is spread in books, in cheap newspapers, by lectures, and the like, and the measures by which this activity should be met on the side of all who are for Religion and for God, should be subjects of earnest thought and meditation for all who have duties which bring them frequently across the evils which have just been enumerated. . . . No one whose occupations lie among considerable numbers of men can pass many days or even many hours without hearing religious subjects discussed, and the discussion will too often take a blasphemous tone. The mechanic, the young man in the house of business, the clerk in the office, however good and sound their faith may be, will often hear statements which they cannot contradict, though they feel them to be false; arguments which they cannot answer, though they know them to be fallacious. It is often the case that such persons have to spend the greater part of their time in company in which irreligious talk is usual or perpetual." ("Month," Sept, 1874.)

Here, then, we have two facts of momentous import staring us in the face; the first is that the British nation is becoming more and more brutalized; and the second is that it is becoming more and more infidel, that it is taking up the Religion of Denial, and rejecting that form of Christianity offered it by Protestantism. I ask calm-judging men whether or not there is a relation of cause and effect between the process of brutalizing and the fundamental principle of the Religion of Denial? I ask them seriously whether or no, if there is no God in Heaven, and if man is merely an expanded mud-fish, with no freedom of will, no spirituality, no responsibility, but with violent lusts and cravings—whether or no, if such be the case, any one in the world can blame him for doing exactly as he likes, and getting as much pleasure, gross or otherwise, as he can compass during his short career on earth —if man be a dog or a hog, why not act as such? What law has to hinder him from seeking to satisfy that particular craving that is strongest, and indulging in that especial excess which gives him the most exquisite delight? I cannot even imagine any reason why he should not; I can see every reason why he should, and every reason why he will and why he does; for if there be no God or Lawgiver, and if man is merely a piece of carbon, how can he help himself, or even dream of doing anything except squeeze the greatest amount of pleasure for himself out of life in the most successful way he can? Brutalization is a direct consequence of the Religion of Denial, as civilization is a direct consequence of the Religion of Affirmation, of the Religion of the Cross. Even the more cunscientious theoretical promoters of the Religion of Denial shrink back, at least at present, from the full consequences of their principles. They are, fortunately, some of them, better than their creed; and have upon them the pressure of that Christian tradition which they cannot throw off, but which, unless something be done, will lose its hold over society more and more every day. So far we may thank the Christianity which still remains to us that things have not progressed still more rapidly than they have towards brutalization.

"The Christianity which yet remains diffused amongst us," says Dr. Mivart, "and the refinement of modern manners, render the open practice of licentiousness and sanguinary rites as yet impossible; but the spirit which prompted them finds in this system of contemporary anti-theists its complete and logical justification, as it has found in a contemporary poet its distinct lyrical expression—the tendency of this movement is to approach little by little to this worst phase of Paganism, as the corruption of morals gradually increases through the temporary decreasing influence of Christianity upon the outer surface of society. Already we have openly advocated the murder of the infirm, the sick, the suffering, the old, as well as self-murder. Free-love has not only its advocates, but its avowed votaries, and a hatred of marriage and the family tie is one of the sentiments common to those political enthusiasts, who claim

for themselves *par excellence* the title of Advanced."
("Contemporary Evolution," pp. 43, 44.) Virchow distinctly tells us that "Socialism," the political expression of the Religion of Denial, is intimately connected with the mud-fish theory of evolution. "Gentlemen," he exclaims to the assembly of German savants, "I will only hope that the evolution theory may not bring upon us all the alarm that similar theories have actually roused in the neighboring country. At all events, this theory, if consistently carried out, has a very serious aspect, and I trust that it has not escaped your notice that Socialism has already established a sympathetic relation with it. We must not conceal these facts from ourselves." ("Freedom of Science," p. 19.)

See now how this principle of the Religion of Denial is corrupting the whole mass of civilized society, society which owes all its moral elevation to the Religion of Affirmation. I do not presume to use my own words to show you this. One has just spoken who sits on the high watch-tower of the world, and takes in, at a glance, the condition of all nations, even of the furtherest from his throne. What has Leo XIII just told the Bishops of the world regarding the present condition of human society? He describes the character of that Religion of Denial, which in point of fact has been evolved from the theory of the mud-fish. His words are too weighty and too important not to be quoted in this connection. He shows clearly which way the world is drifting, having broken loose from the Christian principle, and having adopted that of Unbelief. The very fact of his speaking as he does shows his direct antagonism to it, and its absolute antagonism to him. "As the nature of Our Apostolic office required of Us," he says, "from the very beginning of Our Pontificate, in an Encyclical letter addressed to you, Venerable Brethren, We did not neglect to advert to the deadly pestilence which is creeping through the innermost frame of human society, and brings it into the extremity of danger, and We at the same time pointed out the most efficacious remedies by which it may be restored to health and may escape the very grave dangers which threaten it. But those evils which We then deplored have in a short time increased to such a degree that We are constrained to address you again, the voice of the Prophet, as it were, ringing in Our ears: *Cry aloud and cease not, lift up thy voice like a trumpet.* You will easily understand, Venerable Brethren, that We speak of that sect of men who are called by different and almost barbarous names, Socialist, Communists, or Nihilists, and who, scattered through the whole world, and most closely bound together by most unholy ties, no longer seek safety in the shades of secret assemblies, but, boldly coming forward into the light of day, strive to accomplish the design which they have formed long since of overthrowing the foundations of every civil society. These are they who, as the Divine oracles testify, *defile the flesh, despise dominion and blaspheme majesty.* Nothing which has been wisely enacted by human and Divine laws for the security and adornment of life is left by them intact or entire. They refuse obedience to the higher powers, to which, according to the admonition of the Apostle, every soul ought to be subject, and which derive their right of governing from God, and they preach the perfect equality of all men in rights and offices. They dishonor the natural union of the man and woman, which even barbarous nations hold sacred, and weaken or even sacrifice to lust the bond of that union, by which, principally, domestic society is held together. Allured, moreover, by the desire of present good, which is *the root of all evils and which some coveting have erred from the faith*, they impugn the right of property sanctioned by the Law of Nature, and by a monstrous crime, while they appear to meet the wants and satisfy the desires of all men, they aim at seizing and holding in common whatever has been acquired by the title of lawful inheritance, or by the intellect, or the labor of the hands, or by frugal living. And these portentous opinions they publish in their meetings, inculcate in pamphlets, and scatter among the lower orders in a cloud of journals. From this it results that the reverend majesty and rule of kings has so incurred the hatred of a seditious populace that nefarious traitors, impatient of every restraint, have more than once within a short space of time, in impious daring, turned their arms against the Princes of the realm themselves. But this audacity of perfidious men which threatens greater ruin to civil society, and strikes the minds of all with anxious fear, derives its cause and origin from those poisonous doctrines which, scattered in former times like corrupt seed among the peoples, have borne such pestilential fruit in their season. . . . The object of the war has been that, by setting aside all Revelation, and the subversion of every kind of Supernatural order, an entrance might be cleared for the discoveries, or rather the delirious imaginations of mere Reason. This kind of error, which wrongly usurps the name of Reason, as it entices and sharpens the desire of superiority naturally implanted in man, and gives a loose rein to desires of every kind, has spontaneously penetrated to the widest extent not only very many minds, but civil society itself. Hence it has come to pass that, by a novel impiety, unheard of even among the heathen nations, States have been constituted without taking any account of God and of the order established by Him;

it has been, moreover, declared that public authority derives neither its principle nor its majesty, nor its power of command from God, but rather from the multitude of the people, which, thinking itself absolved from all Divine sanction, has determined to acknowledge only those laws which itself has framed according to its own good pleasure. The supernatural verities of Faith having been impugned and rejected as if they were inimical to reason, the Author and Redeemer Himself of the human race has been insensibly, and, little by little, forcibly banished from the universities, the lyceums, the gymnasiums, and from every public institution connected with the life of man. Finally, the reward and punishment of the future and eternal life being relegated to oblivion, the ardent desire of happiness has been confined within the span of this present life. These doctrines having been disseminated far and wide, this so great license of thought and action being everywhere introduced, it is no wonder that men of the lowest class, weary of a poor home or workshop, should desire to invade the palaces and fortunes of the rich; it is no wonder that there now exists no tranquillity in public or private life, and that the human race has nearly reached its lowest depth." (Given 28 Dec., 1878.)

Well may the very professors of the Religion of Denial groan in spirit when they see their work. "There are few reflective persons," says Bradlaugh, "who have not been, now and again, impressed with awe as they looked back to the past of humanity. . . It is then that we see the grandest illustrations of that unending necessity, under which, it would seem, man labors, necessity of abandoning ever and again the heritage of his fathers, . . . of continually leaving behind him the citadel of faith and peace, raised by the piety of the past, for an atmosphere of tumult and denial. . . . Whatever may be our present conclusions about Christianity, we cannot too often remember that it has been one of the most important factors in the life of mankind." ("National Reformer," Oct. 6 1878.) Listen to the cry of another writer in his agony, who has made shipwreck of his faith. "Does that new philosophy of history," asks Glennie, "which destroys the Christian philosophy of itself afford an adequate basis for such a reconstruction of the ideal as is required? Candidly, we must reply, 'Not yet.' . . . Very far are we from being the first who have experienced the agony of discovered delusion." ("In the Morning Land," p. 29.) "Never in the history of man," says another, "has so terrific a calamity befallen the race, as that which all who look may now behold advancing as a deluge, black with destruction, resistless in might, uprooting our most cherished hopes, engulfing our most precious creed, and burying our highest life in mindless desolation. The floodgates of Infidelity are open, and Atheism overwhelming is upon us. . . . . Man has become in a new sense, the measure of the universe; and in this, the latest and most appalling of his surroundings, indications are returned from the infinite voids of space and time that his intelligence, with all its noble capacities for love and adoration, is yet alone, destitute of kith or kin in all this universe of being. . . . Forasmuch as I am far from being able to agree with those who affirm that the twilight doctrine of the 'new faith' is a desirable substitute for the waning splendor of 'the old,' I am not ashamed to confess that with this virtual negation of God, the universe to me has lost its soul of loveliness. And when at times I think, as think at times I must, of the appalling contrast between the hallowed glory of that creed which once was mine, and the lonely mystery of existence as now I find it, at such times I shall ever feel it impossible to avoid the sharpest pang of which my nature is susceptible." ("Physicus: On Theism." p. 51.)

"We cannot judge of the effects of Atheism," says Sir J. Stephen, "from the conduct of persons who have been educated as believers in God, and in the midst of a nation that believes in God. If we should ever see a generation of men, especially a generation of Englishmen, to whom the word God had no meaning at all, we should get a light upon the subject which might be lurid enough." ("First Principles," p. 117.)

"Few *if any*," even Herbert Spencer says, "are as yet fitted wholly to dispense with such [religious] conceptions as are current. The highest abstractions take so great a mental power to realize with any vividness, and are so inoperative upon conduct unless they are vividly realized, that their regulative effects must for a long period to come be appreciable on but a small minority. . . Those who relinquish the faith in which they have been brought up, for this most abstract faith in which Science and Religion unite, may not uncommonly fail to act up to their convictions. Left to their organic morality, enforced only by general reasoning imperfectly wrought out and difficult to keep before the mind, their defects of nature will often come out more strongly than they would have done under their previous creed." ("Liberty, Equality, and Fraternity," p. 325, 2nd Ed.) In a word, it is as about as easy for the soul and moral sense to live upon abstractions and false maxims as it is for the body to get fat upon thin air. There is a sense within man too strong for all the infidel logic in the world. We know that behind the veil there is One who personally knows and loves us, we know it as surely as that we personally know and love Him in return. We are forced to exclaim, in the words of Lowell:

> God of our fathers, Thou who wast,
> Art, and shall be when the eye-wise who flout
> Thy secret presence shall be lost
> In the great light that dazzles them to doubt,
> We who believe Life's bases rest
> Beyond the probe of chemic test,
> Still, like our fathers, feel Thee near!

And besides this, we know, moreover, that the Religion of Denial, far from being approved of even by those who do not hold with Christianity, is looked upon by the more far-seeing amongst them as a mere empty hypothesis. It is not its truth, but the license it allows that makes it palatable with the multitude. Scientific men themselves, men that is, who are philosophers as well as scientists, are, by their inexorable logic, drawing it down from its pedestal, and displaying it in its veritable colors. Founded on falsehood, it is the fruitful parent of every species of debasement.

Allow me to quote the London *Times*' correspondent, giving a summary of Hackel's teaching, as delivered before the German naturalists in Munich, 1877, and the reply of Virchow. The correspondent says that "having contended that the Biblical account of this planet's creation has long been demolished by geology, Herr Hackel wondered that morphology should have been so slow to come forward and explain the origin and diversity of the animal world. According to him, the two principles of inheritance and adaptation explain the development of the manifold existing organism from a single organic cell; which, were further argument needed to disprove supernatural intervention, we have only to turn to the frequent occurrence of undeveloped and useless organs in many types of the animal world to realize the truth. In this way the Creator is disposed of, not only as superfluous, but as a Being who, if He existed, instead of being all-wise, would every now and then have committed the indiscretion of attempting to create eyes and wings which His power did not suffice to perfect. Then, passing on to the omnipotent cell constituting the groundwork of animal bodies, he referred his audience to certain zoological inquiries proving the possession of motion and sensibility, of perception and will, even by those primary organisms consisting of but a single cell. Everything being thus dependent upon the cell, the lecturer at this stage became interested in the matter forming this marvellous organism. The cell, then, consists of matter called protoplasm, composed chiefly of carbon, with an admixture of hydrogen, oxygen, nitrogen and sulphur. These component parts, properly united, produce the body and soul of the animated world, and, suitably nursed, become man. With this simple argument the mystery of the universe is explained, the Divinity annulled and a new era of infinite knowledge ushered in. It was a fitting conclusion to such a scientific *pronunciamento* that the lecturer, who regarded his argument as incontrovertible, insisted that it should be taught in every school in the land." (The *Times*, Nov. 30, 1877.) Here, then, is Hackel dogmatically laying down a teaching which is subversive of the whole scheme of Natural and Supernatural Religion; here is an "advanced thinker," an Apostle of the Religion of Denial urging that such teaching should be made a portion of the National Education. And here, on the other hand, is another "advanced thinker," absolutely contradicting him, and declaring that Hackel's doctrines are merely "fancies," and not established truths at all.

Listen to Virchow's own words: "It is easy to say that a cell consists of small portions, and these we call *Plastidules*, and that plastidules are composed of carbon, hydrogen, oxygen and nitrogen, and are endowed with an especial soul; which soul is the product of some of the forces which the chemical atoms possess. To be sure this is possible. I cannot form an exact judgment about it. It is one of the positions which are for me still unapproachable. I feel like a sailor who puts forth into an abyss, the extent of which he cannot see. But I must plainly say that, so long as no one can define for me the properties of carbon, hydrogen, oxygen, and nitrogen, in such a way that I can conceive how from the sum of them a soul arises, so long am I unable to admit that we should be at all justified in imparting the 'plastidulic soul' into the course of our education, or in requiring every educated man to receive it as scientific truth so as to argue from it as a logical premiss, and to found his whole view of the world upon it. This we really cannot demand. On the contrary, I am of opinion that, before we designate such hypotheses as the voice of Science —before we say, 'This is modern Science'—we should first have to conduce a long series of elaborate investigations. We must therefore say to the teachers in schools, 'Do not teach it.'" ("Freedom of Science," p. 23, 45.) Farther on he exclaims, after speaking of how Oken taught a doctrine as absolutely true which turned out to be absolutely false: "Gentlemen, let us not fail to profit by the experience of that great naturalist; let us not forget that when the public see a doctrine, which has been exhibited to them as certain, established, positive, and claiming universal acceptance—proved to be faulty in its very foundations, or discovered to be willful and despotic in its essential and chief tendencies, they may lose faith in Science. Then break forth the reproaches: 'Ah, you yourselves are not quite sure; your doctrine, which you call truth to-day, is to-morrow a lie; how can you demand that your teaching should form the subject of education, and a recognized part of our general knowledge?'" (Ibid, p. 41.)

And surely now I have said enough. I have shown you that the fundamental principle on which the Religion of Denial is based leads back logically and inexorably towards that state of bestiality from which "modern thought" says man has sprung. You have seen with your logical eyes that you cannot get more out of a thing than is in it; and if it be really true that there is no God, and that man is simply a mud-fish, that mud-fish never can be blown out into anything higher or better, or more noble than the stuff out of which it comes. A soap-bubble may reflect all the colors of the rainbow, but it will be a soap-bubble still—it will burst when brightest, and you will find there is nothing in it. I have shown you how this bubble of "Denial," whilst pretending to take the place of Christianity, is the absolute death of every moral principle, and of all religion worthy of the name. I have shown you how the cowardly, or at least the unmanly way in which scientific men treat the profoundest questions, creates suspicion; and how others, with less head, but, perhaps, more courage, sweep their cobwebs on one side and boldly deny God's existence altogether. I have drawn your attention to the fact that no sooner is God denied and man declared a mere protoplasm than minds are at once actively engaged in forming plans by means of which they make use of their new freedom from restraint, and indulge in every species of immorality and viciousness, so long as it give them personal pleasure to do so. I have shown you how these teachings inevitably drag the human race down to the very mire; and how philosophers do not shame to suggest to their disciples that the life of a hog is the happiest life for them. I have called your attention to the picture drawn by Thomas Carlyle of "the universal swine's-trough" which man has now to wallow in, that is, if he be true to the Religion of Denial, and to the bestial nature Denial says is his; and I have corroborated, by undeniable statistics, the teaching of Carlyle, showing how the masses of the English people at home are plunging deeper and deeper in brutalization and infidelity as days go by. I have shown you that this is the natural effect of an intelligible cause—of people giving up Christianity and taking to the Religion of Denial, and thus providing for themselves a logical justification for all the enormities which they commit. I have suggested how crime is but the fruit which is produced by the tree of Infidelity; and that unbelief and bestiality are intimately related as cause and as effect. I have shown you, moreover, from Virchow's teaching, that the Religion of Denial and Socialism are in closest sympathy, and, by quoting the words of Pope Leo XIII in his Encyclical, I have drawn your attention to the fact, which anyone can see the truth of at a glance, that the chaos and confusion into which Religion and Civil Society are plunged all over the world are due to the action of that same principle of collapse.

I have suggested that it is Christianity, even in those men who trample on it, which makes them better than their principles, and that still preserves the world from absolute destruction. I have shown how the very champions of the Religion of Denial are terrified by its effect, and cry out in despair that they have been deceived in their anticipations; and, finally, I have called your attention to the curious circumstance that these very champions themselves are fighting with each other; and that what is declared by Hackel to-day to be a victorious discovery of Science is declared by Virchow to-morrow to be a mere craze on his opponent's mind, without any underpin of logic for its support—the very fundamental principle of the Religion of Denial being proved to be no principle at all, but a subjective fancy or maggot in the mind of a naturalist who is possessed by a special anxiety to upset the Christian creed. When to all this is added what I have already proved; that it is reasonable to hold man to be a man, and not a mud-fish; and that there is a God ruling heaven and earth, instead of no God at all; these two facts being substantiated, the very ground has, by the doing so, been cut from under the feet of the Religion of Denial, and it is convicted of being not merely shallow, but a stupid, as well as a deadly poisonous deceit, used by intellectual criminals or by superficial thinkers without sense of responsibility, for upheaving the deep foundations of Supernatural Religion, and of that morality which must ever be synonymous with restraint. I do not dare to trust myself to speak of such men as these, who, by means of a blasphemous and lying philosophy, have brought so much ruin and desolation into the homes of my fellow-men.

Next Sunday I hope to show you the bright side of the picture, for this evening our work has been sad enough. I shall aim at giving you sufficient reason for coming to the conclusion that, whilst the Religion of Denial is shallow and something worse, as has been proved, the Religion of Affirmation, or Christianity, on the other hand, is reasonable, and should be embraced by every sane and prudent man.

FAITH.

Archbishop Vaughan delivered the last of his course of Lenten lectures on Sunday evening, April 6. The usual interest was manifested in it, and there was a very great congregation present. The subject was "Faith." His Grace said :—

We have now come to the beginning of the end. I have, I presume, given sufficient cause to convince men of good will that Unbelief is "shallow," if it be not something very much worse; and, now, I at once proceed to fulfill my promise of showing to those who are seriously and candidly disposed, that Christianity is reasonable; and, therefore, with reason can be adopted as the creed of the prudent and thoughtful.

It will be remembered that at the outset I distinctly declared that I was addressing myself to the living, not to the dead; to the present, not to the future; in one word, to those same fellow-creatures of mine who this moment are energizing in the flesh before us. True, what will fit their case will most probably fit the case of most others, and I may be said roughly to be addressing myself to all mankind; still, I am addressing myself to you, and not to all mankind, for by so restricting myself I am enabled to make my meaning clearer and my argument more forcible. The abstract and indefinite should, as much as can be, be avoided in reasoning; and the concrete and the definite should be seized and dealt with, as much as possible, in its place. It is by so doing that argument is driven home, and living men and women are made to feel the impress and the despotic power of Truth.

Having, then, during the last few Sunday nights, been drawn towards the conclusion that you are rational beings created by God, endowed with spirituality and responsibility; having come to the conclusion that it is reasonable to believe in the soul and in the Sovereign Creator and Master, having thus been brought into immediate contact, as it were, with the Great Supreme, you exclaim spontaneously with the poet:

God is law, say the wise, O soul, and let us rejoice;
For, if He thunder by law, the thunder is yet His voice.
Speak to Him, thou, for He hears, and Spirit with spirit may
    meet;
Closer is He than breathing, and nearer than hands and feet.

Having thus far advanced towards the threshold of my main contention, it remains now to make another, and, it would seem, a longer stride in advance, and show not merely the reasonableness of Theism, but, what is much more, the reasonableness of Christianity itself. And how do I set about doing this with such scanty admissions as I have asked for from you? and after having advanced so short a distance along the road towards the reception of so many tenets and dogmatic decisions as are embraced in the Christian code?

I set about it in this way. I appeal to your own consciences and sense; and I ask you, as living men and women of good will, to turn your thoughts for a moment upon yourselves. You have sufficient reason for believing that you are what I have said you are; you have sufficient reason for believing in a God who made you, loves you, and who, therefore, must be very near to every one of you, for you know that He has written His Natural Law in your consciences, and that He has given you a keen sense of right and wrong. Now, I ask, such being the case, is it unreasonable to suppose that God has done something more than this? Would He leave man alone in the midst of the fog and obscurity of life, and give him no further help than the light of reason and the guide of conscience? Is not life too filled with confusion and the path too difficult and the way too dark for man to be left absolutely to himself without any further help than that provided in the natural order? Dr. Newman expresses my meaning when he says: "Starting with the being of a God, . . I look out of myself into the world of men, and there I see a sight which fills me with unspeakable distress. The world seems simply to give the lie to that great truth, of which my whole being is so full; and the effect upon me is, in consequence, as a matter of necessity, as confusing as if it denied that I am in existence myself. If I looked into a mirror and did not see my face, I should have the sort of feeling that actually comes upon me when I look into this living, busy world, and see no reflection of its Creator. This is to me one of the greatest difficulties of this absolute primary truth to which I referred just now. Were it not for this voice, speaking so clearly in my conscience and in my heart, I should be an Atheist, or a Pantheist, or a Polytheist, when I looked into the world." Again: "To consider the world in its length and breadth, its various history, the many races of man, their starts, their fortunes, their mutual alienation, their conflicts, and then their ways, habits, governments, forms of worship, their enterprises, their aimless courses, their random achievements and acquirements, the impotent conclusion of long-standing facts, the tokens so faint and broken of a superintending design, the blind evolution of what turns out to be great powers or truths, the progress of things, as if from unreasoning elements, not towards final causes, the greatness and littleness of man, his far-reaching aims, his short duration, the curtain hung over his futurity, the disappointments of life, the defeat of good, the success of evil, physical pain, mental anguish, the prevalence and intensity of sin, the pervading idolatries, the corruptions, the dreary irreligion, that condition of the whole race, so hopeless, so fearfully yet so exactly described in the Apostles words, 'having no hope, and without God in the world,'—all this is a vision to dizzy and appall, and inflicts upon the mind the sense of a profound mystery which is absolutely beyond human solution." (See "Apologia," also " Grammar of Assent," pp. 391-394.)

Such being the condition of the world in which you live, and the darkness surrounding you, which of yourselves you cannot fathom, does not that same conscience, which suggests to you the Being of a God; His love and mercy suggest also to you that He would not have left you wholly to yourselves, but would have given you some guiding light? The poet brings out my meaning when he says to the bird flying solitarily away to sea:

    Whither, midst falling dew,
While glow the heavens with the last steps of day,
Far through their rosy depths dost thou pursue
    Thy solitary way?

    There is a power who care
Teaches thy way along the pathless coast,
The desert and illimitable air,
    Lone wandering, but not lost.

> He who, from zone to zone,
> Guides through the boundless sky thy certain flight
> In the lone way that I must tread alone,
> Will lead my steps aright.

How, then, does he lead our "steps aright?" Has he made any provision for this? Who are you? What has He done? You are reasonable, responsible beings who have reached a certain point in your career onwards. You have each your history. You have each had, we will suppose, a fair education; and are, in the main, I think I may say, actively engaged in the affairs of life. Few amongst you, I take it, have been brought up as trained theologians or philosophers; but, like the vast majority of mankind, you have learnt your religion from those who went before you, and have lived, in the main, through the traditions of the past. You do not call yourselves religious experts. And thus you represent what may be called Christian civilization, which is perpetuated on the earth, one generation gradually disappearing as another gradually grows into its place and inherits its traditions. Such being the case, what more has God done for you besides giving you a reasoning faculty and the *sensus numinis?* How will you answer this question? You will assuredly look out from your conscience abroad upon the world in which you live; you will ask whether or no the Almighty has left any tokens or foot-prints of Himself down the history of time; whether there is any record of His especial dealings with your forefathers and with yourselves, which is over and above His action in your conscience; and which does not cross its dictates, but supplements and develops them. Here, then, you at once come into the practical region of living facts and incontrovertible history, which, in their sphere, bear as powerful a witness as the conscience itself to moral and religious truth. Looking, then, out into the world, you see all that confusion which Dr. Newman so graphically describes. You find the human intellect more busy than ever in uprooting ancient landmarks. You perceive, to use the words of Cardinal Guibert, in an address connected with the opening of the French Senate this very year (January 8), that: "We are passing through a profoundly troublous period, in which people appear to be no longer cognizant of even the most common principles or laws of equity and reason. The most difficult problems are dealt with without any precaution; foundations of society are removed by the most rash discussions; religion, the family, education, authority, property, all are called in question with incredible levity by men frequently of moderate ability, of no experience, and of very doubtful education." You become aware that Science itself is debased and dishonored by men who either fear to tell their minds or who drag it into the arena as a vulgar controversial weapon, and thus injure a high and noble instrument of knowledge and civilization. You cannot help seeing, to use the words of Mivart, that "A passionate hatred of religion, however discreetly or astutely veiled, lies at the bottom of much of the popular metaphysical teaching now in vogue. A belief in the necessary inconsistency of Science with Religion is therefore persistently propagated among the public by writings and lectures in which more is implied than asserted. In such lectures, attempts have again and again been made to strike Theology through Physical Science, to blacken Religion with coal dust, to pelt it with fragments of chalk, or to smother it with sub-Atlantic mud, or to drown it in a sea of protoplasm. *Delenda est Carthago!* No system is to be tolerated which will lead men to accept a personal God, moral responsibility, and a future state of rewards and punishments. Let these unwelcome truths be once eliminated, and no system is deemed undeserving of a candid, if not sympathetic, consideration, and, *cæteris paribus*, that system which excludes them most efficaciously becomes the most acceptable." ("Lessons from Nature," chap. xiii, p. 240.)

You have seen that with all their boasting, and in spite of all their caution and cunning, Atheists, disguised as scientific men, have not only propounded as true that which is false or merely hypothetical, but that their fundamental principle leads to the most revolting brutality, and is destructive not simply of morality and religion, but of all and every initial sense of right and wrong. What guide, then, if any, have you, I ask, in the midst of all this confusion that troubles your conscience so, and bewilders your reason? Looking out from myself into the world in the midst of all this dizzying whirl and moving chaos, I perceive two principles at work distinct as the principle of Denial and Affirmation. The civilized world, which, in the main, believes in God and conscience, declares to me that God has done something more than give man a natural conscience and the light of reason; it as firmly declares that He has given a revelation of His will, teaching man what to believe with his intellect, and what to do in consequence of that belief. If man fulfill that will and law of God, he will be forever happy; if he die in grave prevarication, he will be forever punished. Without going into the reasons of this—such is the belief of the great civilized Christian world into which I have been born. This Revelation of God's will is said to be, at least in part, contained in a book called the "Bible"; and the whole Christian world, of 407 millions of human beings, holds this book to be inspired, and the great cardinal truths contained in it of Christ's dignity to be true also. Thus I find, without going into the merits of the case, that the most civilized and intelligent peoples in the world, the sovereign race, believe in the broad basis of the Christian scheme.

But, after having taken this general view, and looked a little closer, I find one radical and fundamental difference. I find this vast mass of believers divided by a sharp line of principle, which cuts them, as with a knife, in two, and throws them into opposition. I find one smaller mass of believers basing their teaching, or rather their personal faith, on what they call private judgment or individual fancy, and another, much larger mass, basing theirs on authority. Which is the more reasonable and safe, as a guide to wandering humanity—to put the Book in each one's hand and say: "Do your best and make out God's will and law for yourself from this?" or to say: "Here is the Book; you wish to know God's law and will. I am commissioned to teach it to you: I cannot lead you astray in faith and morals; and if you follow my living voice, you will be safe?" I, who know something of struggling humanity, cannot but think it a mockery to hand the Book to each one, and tell each to do the best he can with it for himself. "Here is the Bible; take it, read it, learn God's will from it!"—to whom is such a command addressed? I will reply in the words of a clever writer, who has known something of the struggles of human kind: "First, they are addressed to the thousands, the millions of workingmen and women, who eat their bread in the sweat of their brow. They are addressed to the illiterate poor in the cities, in the fields, in the factories, in the docks, in the mines, to the men and women who cannot read, or, if they can read, who cannot put a premise to a premise; and who, even if they could read and could reason, have to work hard from morning till night. What mockery to tell a workingman, an anxious bread-winner of a family, who walks out to his work in the morning hardly refreshed, and comes home at night tired out with toil, what a mockery to tell him he must devote his mind to find out whether or not he has a soul, whether or not that soul is immortal, and what the future life is likely to be! Hard, grinding labor from the morning when they rise, reluctant and slow, to the evening when they sink down again weary and overcome, to eat and then to sleep—is this a school where men can settle the deepest questions of speculative truth? And if you rise in the scale of intelligence, and take a class that is better off and has more leisure, the mockery is still the same. Look through all the grades of the great middle class, from the well-to-do artisan to the banker and professional man; think how full of work their life is, how busy their brains and their hands; remember how, in every great country, it is a condition of greatness that the immense majority of the citizens dedicate their best and longest hours to the production of wealth in one shape or another; consider, among all the clever and educated men who make up the very marrow of our national life, how difficult it is to find one whom you would trust to give you a decided answer to an unprofessional speculative question, such as, for instance, in what circumstance it is permissible to take another man's property; and then say whether it be not a wild delusion to suppose that, from these busy workers, can come any clear or consistent system of natural theology or natural law. . . . Invite them to prove the existence of God in the midst of an Atheistic generation, and you mock them. Their minds are full of money;

they have ventures at home and abroad; they discuss
companies, and harvests, and mines; they think of digging
and moulding and making; they watch the skies; they are
intent upon the field and upon the beast; they handle the
fruits of the earth; or, perchance, they study the schemes
of princes and parliaments, the fever of nations, the dis-
turbances of peoples and the fluctuations of funds; or, it
may be, that they pore with close and eager eye over the
secret of Science; or take the pen and make books; or
seek their gain and their fame in the arduous practice of
exacting professions; in a word, they are the men who
make the cabinets of governments, who fills the halls of
Justice, of Science, of Commerce, who work the banks
and the printing-presses of this unresting world. Teach
them, bring your truth to their doors, and they will look
at it. . . . But do not mock them by asking them
to supply a darkened world with its necessary light."
(Bishop Hedley's "Light of the Holy Spirit," p. 9.)
Thus I find it self-evident that the Book and individual
fancy does not answer to the wants of struggling humanity.
My reason is not satisfied with this method, even supposing
all could study the Book and made a religion out of it.

For, on looking closer still, I find another most painful
fact exhibiting itself on a large scale, namely, that that
very Book which was to bring unity of faith and oneness
of moral teaching, has been, under this system, the prolific
parent of hundreds of contradictory creeds:

> This is the Book where each his dogma seeks,
> And this the Book where each his dogma finds.

In a word, I discover, looking out on the broad world, that
two incontrovertible facts stare me straight in the face:
first, that the vast majority of mankind have not capacity

or time for forming their religion out of the Book, and, secondly, that those who imagine they have, are set at once in perfect contrast and contradiction in fundamental points of religious teaching. Of those who adopt the radical principle of individual fancy, each man choosing the religion he most approves, or, on the same principle, rejecting Religion altogether, there are said to be 71 millions in Europe, divided into various organizations or sects, all of which maintain that they may, after all, be teaching absolute error, so far as they are teaching anything at all; each and all being unable, if they are consistent with their fundamental principle, to condemn any man, even should he declare it to be his candid opinion that all religion and morality are absurd, and that the Religion of Denial is the only sensible creed for honest men, and that each man has his own head, and he must use it for himself. At a modest computation we are assured that in England alone there are at least 150 independent sects, each held together by an independent organization, and each considering its own form of Christianity most conformable to the Divine ideal. Outside of these there is the Church of England with its 23,000 clergymen.

To illustrate the working of the fundamental principle of individual fancy, allow me to quote the opinions expressed by Non-conformist organs regarding that said Church, with its 23,000 clergymen. "Cathedrals," they say, "are not, in any sense of the word, missionary colleges; there is no 'diligent' preaching of the Gospel from them. . . A heavy langour lies over nearly all cathedral cities, . . and the grossest immoralities find in that stagnant air a cause and an encouragement." "There is probably no body of men in the world, who, so far as outward evidence goes, care less for the furtherance of Religion than the

English (Protestant) Bishops." "It is notorious that many persons are living in adultery because of their inability to pay the fee demanded by the clergyman." "The clergy identify themselves with simony. .... The Bishops make no objection to it." "To raven like a wolf, and to plunder like a freebooter, has been the peculiar prerogative of the Church of England." "There is no sect so schismatical, so unbrotherly, so insultingly unfraternal, as the Episcopalians. Her Canons remain to this very hour the very quintessence of bigotry; their spirit is, to put it plainly, infernal." You will find this question fully treated in the *Quarterly Review* of January, of the current year, where the above quotations may be found at pages 53 and 54. As to the justice of these remarks, I have nothing to say, except that possibly all these profligate Bishops and parsons are nothing more nor less than Jesuits in disguise! (A visible ripple of amusement passed across the vast audience at this point.) But my point is this, that the principle of Individual Fancy necessarily leads to chaos. Even taking the Anglican Church itself, Macaulay defines it as being not so much a church as an hundred sects battling within one church.

The Anglican *Church Times* (Feb. 1875,) says: "The clergy are, in round numbers, about 23,000. Of these, fully one-half, say 12,000, belong to the High Church school in all its shades and degrees. Twelve of the Bishops may, on a very liberal estimate, be similarly classed. The Evangelical clergy, on their own computation, are about 5,000 in numbers, and have six Bishops definitely on their side, besides two more on whose alliance they can usually count. The Broad Church clergy have, perhaps, but doubtfully, a thousand members, with the Primate and four other Bishops to support them. The unclassifiable and colorless, inclusive of the mere Establishmentarians, mainly absorb the remaining five thousand, and can boast the Archbishop of York and the remaining prelates as partaking their moral weight and influence." It is not necessary for me to go further into this thread-bare subject, so obvious in its results. The more I study the fundamental principle on which the smaller mass of Christians rest, so much the more I find insuperable objections against it, as being a principle that is absolutely unworkable and wholly unfitted to subserve the requirements of the vast majority of men; whilst, when set in motion at all, it produces, as a necessary consequence of its intrinsic nature, not unity and harmony, but violent contrast and everlasting dislocation in the very fundamentals of Religion and Natural Morality, breaking up the very machinery of which it is supposed to form a part, offering no protection against the most pestilential doctrines of the Religion of Denial. I know that many good and conscientious men base their religion on this principle. I am not speaking of men, but of a system, and from that I shrink. I do not dare to

> Tempt with wondering feet
> The dark, unbottomed, infinite abyss,

into which I should have to plunge, and into which so many of my fellow-men have plunged, "deeper than did ever plummet sound," never to rise up again with any clear and definite creed whose truth they could hold to with a sovereign and absolute conviction.

I turn, then, dissatisfied, as a philosopher and a man of the world, from the fundamental principle of individual fancy to the fundamental principle of Authority, on which is based the teaching of the vast majority of civilized mankind. And whilst I am turning round to do so, I hear a multitude of voices crying out that I am a slave and a fool; that to give up your private judgment is handing yourself over, body and soul, to bondage, and that "Britons never shall be slaves." I hear them; I listen attentively; I am on my guard. And thus forewarned, I cautiously study the principle of Authority, not, indeed from Catholic or Protestant divines, but from the writings of laymen of acknowledged genius; men of the world, who hold, or have held, first places for intellect, and who are known to possess an intense love of liberty, and a detestation of all things in the shape of slavery. I will open the writings of Sir George Cornwall Lewis, and of Mr. Gladstone, and see what they teach with regard to the principle of Authority, and the range of it. They shall tell me, unbiassed except as against Catholicity, what the habit of mankind is with regard to the use of other men's knowledge, and as to the amount of reasonable trust men may, and, indeed, are obliged to place in it, and I shall thus discover the bearings of that same principle upon that which is of deepest import, namely, on the present duties of Faith and Action, and the future happiness of man. Let us see whether Authority is synonymous with Despotism, and trust to it a species of miserable serfdom only practiced by miserable Roman Catholics in matters of Religion:—

"The fact to which we ought to be alive," says Mr. Gladstone, "but for the most part are not, is that the whole human family, and the best and highest races of it, and the best and highest minds of those races are to a great extent upon crutches, the crutches which Authority has lent them. Even in the days of Bacon, even in the days of Dante, when knowledge, as the word is commonly understood, was so limited that some elect minds of uncommon capacity and vigor could grasp the whole mass of it, they still depended largely upon authority. For that aggregate of knowledge, which they were able to grasp, was but book-knowledge, and not source-knowledge. It was to a great extent not knowledge of subjects, but of what specially qualified men had said upon subjects. As we now stand, no individual man holds, or can hold, that relation to universal knowledge, which was held by Dante, or by Bacon, or by Leibnitz. A few subjects, in most cases a very few indeed, are or ever can be known in themselves by direct and immediate study; a larger number by an immediate knowledge of what writers, or the most accredited writers, have said upon them ; the largest number by far only from indirect accounts, or as it were, rumors of the results which writers and students have attained.

Ad nos vix tenuis famæ pertabitur aura.

"It seems, however, safe to say that the largest part even of civilized nations, in the greater proportion of the subjects that pass through the mind, or touch the course of common action, have not even this, but have only a vague unverified impression that the multitude, or the best, think so and so, and they had better act and think accordingly.

"Authority, in matters of opinion, divides itself (say) into three principal classes. There is the authority of witnesses. They testify to matters of fact : the judgment upon these is commonly, though not always, easy ; but this testimony is always the substitution of the faculties of others for our own, which, taken largely, constitutes the essence of Authority. This is the kind which we justly admit with the smallest jealously. . . . Then there is the authority of judges. To such authority we have constantly to submit. And this, too, is done for the most part willingly ; but unwillingly when we have been told what we are about. These judges sometimes supply us with opinions upon facts, sometimes with facts themselves. The results, in pure science, are accepted by us as facts; but on the methods by which they are reached, the mass, even of intelligent and cultivated men, are not competently informed. Judgments on difficult questions on finance are made into compulsory laws in parliament, where only one man in a score, possibly no more than one in a hundred, thoroughly comprehends them. All kinds of professional advice belong to this order in the classification of Authorities." Having touched upon the third class of Authority, Mr. Gladstone continues: " While the naked exhibition of the amount of guidance found for us by Authority is certainly unflattering, it has a moral use in the inculcation of much humility. It also offers to the understanding a subject of profound and wondering contemplation, by revealing to us, in measureless extent, the law of human independence, which again should have its moral use in deepening the sense of brotherhood in man.

" A general revolt, then, against Authority, even in matters of opinion, is *a childish and anile superstition*, not to be excused by the pretext that it is only due to the love of freedom cherished to excess. The love of freedom is an essential principle of healthy human action, but is only one of its essential principles. Such a superstition, due only to excess in the love of freedom, may remind us that we should be burned to cinders were the earth capable of imitating its wayward denizens, and indulging itself only in an excess of the centripetal force. We may indeed allow that, when personal inquiry has been thorough, unbiassed and entire, it seems a violation of Natural Law to say that the inquirer should put it aside in deference to others, even of presumably superior qualifications. . . . But the number of the cases in which a man can be sure that his own inquiry fulfills these conditions is comparatively insignificant. Whenever it falls short of fulfilling them, what may be called the subjective speciality of duty disappears; there remains only the paramount law of allegiance to Objective Truth, and that law, commonly dealing with Probable Evidence, binds us to take not that evidence with which we ourselves have most to do, but that which, whether our own or not, offers the smallest among the several likelihoods of error." So it seems, after all the wild talk of the advocates of " Private Judgment," that those very same advocates have been trusting to and living on Authority, I may say almost exclusively, in matters of worldly moment all their lives. Why so sensitive to being slaves in the paramount and most difficult subject of Religion, and so case-hardened as not even to know you are "slaves" in almost everything else? But to leave generalities, let us see how these thoughts about Authority bear upon Religion.

Sir George Lewis, in his "Essay on the Influence of Authority in Matters of Opinion" (London, 2d Edit., 1875), makes several very profound remarks regarding the influence and extensive action of Authority in human affairs. Mr. Gladstone speaks of him as "that learned, modest, most dispassionate and most able man," and refers with evident pleasure to his "remarkable sobriety, his abhorrence of paradox, his indifference to ornament," and to " his rigidly conscientious handling" of his subject. Allow me to make use, as far as they will go, of the teachings of these two keen intelligences, in order that I may bring out as clearly as possible the fundamental principle of the Catholic Church, as distinguished from that of all denominations that surround her. She claims to be a living Teacher, and to teach unadulterated Religious Truth. She speaks with Authority, and she is obeyed, because she is said to have proved herself possessed of the right to speak. This claim is called by some an act of tyranny; and those who oppose her teaching do so on the ground that each man must think for himself and choose for himself, and that no authority should dare to dictate to anyone what to believe and what to do.

Now, using the light given us by two of our keenest English minds—the late Sir George Lewis and Mr. Gladstone—a light all the more valuable because it was not created for the special purpose to which I am applying it—we shall see how far the great-master principle of Catholicism is reasonable and deserves the approval of every calm and unprejudiced mind. Mr. Gladstone evidently fully appreciates the weight of the popular prejudice against believing on "Authority," for in his review of Lewis "Essay," he starts with giving it one or two keen slashes with his controversial sword. He says: "Many are the tricks of speech; and it has become almost a commonplace of our time to set up, in matters of opinion, an opposition between Authority and Truth, and to treat them as excluding one another. It would be about as reasonable to set up an opposition between butchers' meat and food." Again: "Now, it would sound strangely in our ears were any one of the most distinguished dealers in commonplace instead of proclaiming, 'not Authority, but Truth,' to take for his text, 'not Examination, not Inquiry, but Truth.' We should at once reply that Examination or Inquiry was no more in conflict with Truth than our road to London is in conflict with London. The cases are parallel. Inquiry is a road to Truth, and Authority is a road to Truth. Identical in aim, diverse in means and in effect, both resting on the same basis."

Now, what is the conduct of men in the most important affairs of life regarding the use they make of Authority? Do they with consistent determination steadily decline its services, considering that not to do so would be the same as selling themselves into slavery? Do they fall back at once on the principle that "Britons never shall be slaves?" What do Lewis and Gladstone teach the English-speaking public on this point? Lewis says that, "A large proportion of the general opinions of mankind are derived merely from Authority, and the advice of competent judges has great influence in questions of practice. What truths have been discovered by original inquirers, and received by competent judges, it is principally by Authority that they are accredited and diffused." Regarding the way in which opinions are held wholesale simply on the basis of authority, Mr. Gladstone summarizes Lewis' teaching to this effect: "They are such," he says, "as we derive from instruction in childhood, or from seniors or from fashion. He (Lewis) shows the extremely limited power of inquiry by the working class; and how even the well-informed rely chiefly on compendia and secondary authorities. He shows how, in strict truth, when we act upon conclusions of our own, for which the original reasons are no longer present to our minds, we become *authorities* to ourselves; and the direct action of reason is as much ousted, as if we were acting on some authority extrinsic to us. Then there is the deference shown in the region of practice to professional or specially instructed persons; or to friends having experience, which enables a man to discern grounds of unbelief invisible to the unpracticed eye." . . . "In general, it may be said that the authority of the professors of any science is trustworthy in proportion as the points of agreement among them are numerous and important, and the points of difference few and unimportant. . . The opposition which is sometimes made between Authority and Reason rest on a confusion of thought."

Now, with regard to Religion, Lewis expresses the following convictions, or, to use the words of Mr. Gladstone: "The candor, acumen, breadth and attainments of Lewis give a great weight to the convictions he has expressed. They may be summed up in a few words, as follows:—

"1. The consent of mankind binds us in reason to acknowledge the being of God.

"2. The consent of civilized mankind similarly binds us to the acceptance of Christianity.

"3. The details of Christianity are contested; but, in doubtful questions, the Church, and, *e. g.*, the Church of England at large, with respect to its own members, is more competent than they are individually; and the business and duty of a reasonable man, so far as in these matters he is bound to have an opinion, is to follow the best opinion."

Now, Mr. Gladstone, taking the principles laid down by Lewis, gives them a wider extension still; and after I have shown you what that extension is, I shall proceed to make it evident to reasonable men that they can, also, with very good cause, be applied to that one legitimate exponent of historical Christianity which we call the Catholic Church.

"In the first place," says Mr. Gladstone, "belief in God implies much more than that He is superhuman and imperceptible. It seems to involve:

"1. That He is conceived of as possessing in Himself all attributes whatsoever which conduce to excellence, and these in a degree indefinitely beyond the power of the human mind to measure.

"2. Over and above what He is Himself, He is conceived of as standing in certain relations to us, as carrying on a moral government of the world.

"3. The same wide consent of mankind, which sustains belief in a God, and invests Him with a certain character, has everywhere perceptibly . . . carried the sphere of the moral government which it assigns to Him beyond the limits of the visible world. . . .

"4. Along, therefore, with belief in God, we have to register the acknowledgment of another truth, the doctrine of a future state of man, which has had a not less ample acceptance in all quarters from whence the elements of Authority can be drawn." Mr. Gladstone continues: "As we found, in the prior instance of simple Theism, that the authority of consent would carry us much beyond the acknowledgment of a disembodied abstraction, so, upon examining the case of Christianity, we shall find that what has been handed down to us under that name as part of the common knowledge and common patrimony of men is not a bare skeleton, but is instinct with vital warmth from a centre, and has the character, notwithstanding all the dissensions that prevail, of a living and working system not without the most essential feature of an unity.

"This I shall endeavor to show as to the following points:—

"1. The Doctrine of Revelation.
"2. The Use of Sacraments.
"3. The Christian Ethics.
"4. The Creed.
"5. The Doctrines of the Trinity and the Incarnation."

Time does not permit me to quote Mr. Gladstone's proofs regarding the general acceptance of the above. My point is, that in so far as they are accepted by the vast mass, not of the Catholic world alone, but of the Protestant world—

consisting of very self-contradictory Britons "who never will be slaves"—so far, I say, as they are so accepted, they must be, they cannot be otherwise accepted than on Authority. How many of the 71 millions of Protestants can lay their hands on their breasts and say: "I accept those tenets because I have come to the conclusion from my own personal reading and study that they are God's truth?" How many would have had time, or ability, or training, to fit them for such a superhuman task? Surely, so infinitesimal a number, that they would represent little more than a drop in the ocean of mankind. Thus those who are ever declaiming with such incontinence of expression against accepting Religion on Authority, are the very ones to do what they so violently condemn, and become slaves to a system which professes that it is not capable of preventing itself from leading men into the ditch. Myself, I should feel rather shy of joining a body of men who boasted in rather a noisy way that they detested a certain principle of action, and then were convicted immediately of abidingly acting upon it in the most momentous affairs of life and of religion, without entertaining a suspicion of the fact themselves. I should prefer a set of men who, whilst they firmly held a certain principle to be true and sound in the practice of their lives, most carefully and conscientiously conform their actions to it.

Now, if there be such men who do thus act, where are they to be found? They compose that much larger mass of which I spoke. There are 230 or 250 millions of them in the world, all uniting in one creed, in the same sacraments and sacrifice, and all submitting to the authority of one Head, whom they hold to be infallible, under certain conditions, in his teaching on faith and morals.

Let us, then, now turn to this great society which baset

its teaching on a living voice and ever boasts of doing so, and see how far reason concurs in the principle which is adopts. To use the words of an unbeliever, who, though a professed sceptic, looks on things with the eyes of a philosopher. "The Roman Church," says he, "exists, and exists as a power in the world; and, whether she be an enemy to be destroyed or a saviour to be clung to, it is equally important that we should estimate her full strength. It is idle to waste our arguments and our sarcasms on Protestantism only. If we think that Christianity is false, and is doing an evil work in the world, let us meet it and combat it in its strongest and most coherent form. The Church will not shrink from these attacks, she will rather court them. Only see me, she says, what I really am, and then strike me as forcibly as you will or can.

"*Me, me—adsum qui feci—in me convertite ferrum.*"

Let us look, then, for a moment at the position which the Catholic Church holds in the civilized world, and then we shall be better able to judge of her claims on the submission of reasonable men who seek the truth that they may embrace it.

Take the statements of Draper, a deadly enemy to Catholicity. He says: "It is estimated that the entire population of Europe is about three hundred and one millions. Of these, one hundred and eighty-five millions are Roman Catholics, thirty-three millions are Greek Catholics. Of Protestants, there are seventy-one millions, separated into many sects. . . The whole of Christian South America is Roman Catholic; the same may be said of Central America and of Mexico, as also of the Spanish and French West India possessions. . . . The Roman Catholic Church is the most widely-diffused and the most powerfully-organized of all modern societies. . . . It is plain, therefore, that of professing Christians the vast majority are Catholic; and such is the authoritative demand of the Papacy for supremacy, that, in any survey of the present religious condition of Christendom, regard must be mainly had to its acts. Its movements are guided by the highest intelligence and skill. Catholicism obeys the orders of one man, and has, therefore, a unity, a compactness, a power which Protestant denominations do not possess. Moreover, it derives inestimable strength from the souvenirs of the great name of Rome. Unembarrassed by any hesitating sentiment, the Papacy has contemplated the coming intellectual crisis. It has pronounced its decision, and occupied what seemed to it to be the most advantageous ground." ("The Conflict between Religion and Science," p. 329.)

And what Draper says in his book is confirmed by the eye-witness of a Baptist minister, Dr. Potter, of the Sixth street Baptist Church, New York, when giving an account to his congregation of his tour in Europe, spoke as follows: "It has been asserted for many years that the Roman Church is losing its power over the masses of Europe, but this is not so. Romanism is not dead; I candidly believe that it has just begun to live. Its power, vigor and life are manifested in many things. They are seen in its vast cathedrals and in the hastening of long-delayed works. During the last ten years $2,000,000 have been spent on the Cathedral of Cologne, under the especial patronage of the King of Prussia. Throughout Europe I expected to see nothing but decay, but I was greatly disappointed. The power and vitality of the Romish Church are further shown in the great congregations that gather in its places of worship, in the exhibition of a true Catholic spirit, and in the wonderful adaptation of the Church to the necessities of the times and to modern methods of work. . . . Protestantism in its aggressive work does not anywhere show such proofs of foresight, earnestness and devotion as does the Catholic Church." In fact, we have merely to take the ordinary statistics to discover the vitality and spring of life in the Church in the freest countries of the world. Look at its growth in North America. The first priest in the country was ordained at Baltimore in 1793. In 1840 there were 24 Bishops, 629 priests, and 1,751,000 laity; in 1878 there were one Cardinal, eleven Archbishops, 56 Bishops, 7,329 priests, whilst the Catholic population amounted to 7,844,166. In the United States alone there are 5,500 churches, 21 theological seminaries, and 1,121 ecclesiastical students, not to speak of colleges, academies, monasteries and convents in their hundreds.

Now look at the vitality of Catholicity from another point of view. The Faith was carried to America, and has, in the midst of free institutions, flourished with an extraordinary development; but has it the power of recovering lost ground, of coming to life again where it has been trodden into the earth, and all but exterminated out of the land? Allow me to read you an account of the condition of Catholicity in England within the memory of living man, and then to point out to you how marvellously it has sprung up again since those days, with a power which of itself speaks of the influence of Truth. "My Fathers and Brothers," says Dr. Newman in his "Second Spring," "you have seen it (the Catholic position in England) on one side, and some of us on another; but one and all of us can bear witness to the fact of the utter contempt into which Catholicism had fallen by the time that we were born. . . . . No longer the Catholic Church in the country; nay, no longer, I may say, a Catholic community,

but a few adherents of the Old Religion, moving silently
and sorrowfully about, as memorials of what had been.
'The Roman Catholics' not a sect, not even an interest, as
man conceived of it, not a body, however small, representative of the Great Communion abroad, but a mere handful
of individuals who might be counted, like the pebbles and
detritus of the great deluge. . . . . Such were the
Catholics in England found in corners. in alleys, and
cellars, and the house-tops, or in the recesses of the
country; cut off from the populous world around them,
and dimly seen, as if through a mist or in twilight, as
ghosts flitting to and fro, by the high Protestants, the lords
of the earth." (Sermons, "Second Spring," p. 171.)
Such was Catholicity in England some few years since.
What is its position now? At its head is a Cardinal of the
Holy Roman Church, once a Protestant Archdeacon; he
rules over a hierarchy of some thirteen Bishops. There
are, up and down the country at this hour, over 1,900
priests; in 1875, there were over 300 monasteries and
convents, and a large and increasing population of earnest
and devout believers. That the vital principle of Catholicity is remarkably active, and is absorbing into itself some
of the purest and most cultivated English men and women,
is evident to any one who gives a cursory glance at the list
of converts in the *Whitehall Review.* A great change
within the memory of living man! No sooner had the
foot of oppression been removed than the Church rose up
again, and is beginning to assert and effectually to extend
her sway. It cannot be love of power, or wealth, or name,
or fame, that made these men and women abandon their
past lives and begin the world anew. Principle and the
light of Truth alone could have produced these effects.
"It could not well be love of power," says the *Whitehall*

Reviewer, "or of fame, that led Dr. Newman to exchange Oxford that adored him for the Birmingham that knows him not; that tempted Cardinal Manning to step aside from the open path that led easily on to Lambeth Palace and a seat in the Lords; that weighed with a hundred rectors and vicars, such as Oakeley and Faber and Bathurst, who left fat livings and certain promotion to labor as obscure parish priests amongst the ignorant and the poor; that brought the noblest of earth's sons and daughters, with such title as Norfolk, Argyll, Buccleuch, Hamilton, Ripon, Bute, Londonderry, Lothian, Queensberry, Denbigh, Gainsborough and Herbert, to bow before the lowliest ministers of the lowly; or that led poets like Coventry Patmore and Aubrey de Vere to adopt a creed that put them out of harmony with the temper of their time. It was not 'love of ecclesiasticism' that made Henry Wilberforce, Edward Walford, Lord Charles Thynne, Mr. Oxenham, and a hundred more, leave the care of souls in the Anglican system to join a Church where, from one cause or another, they could never rise above the level of the laity. It was no want of learning or disinclination to weigh evidence that led men like the author of 'The Apologia,' and Mr. Allies, after years of controversy, to change one creed for another. Pecuniary gain could hardly be the ground on which clergymen with wives and families gave up their emoluments to fight against starvation as best they could with strange weapons, which one, at least, to our certain knowledge, wielded so ill that he sought at last for shelter in a workhouse; and love of money cannot be the conduct-guage of a company that includes Thomas Henry, who became a priest of the old faith rather than a wordling millionaire, and George Lane Fox, the eldest son of Yorkshire's greatest gentleman, the

Squire of Braham, of whose enthusiastic zeal and charity his co-religionists are proud to speak."

It is evident, without words, that there must have been something very potent in Catholicism to induce these and thousands more to make the great wrench of breaking with the past and of embarking anew in the battle of life. No philosopher with any power of insight could resist the natural temptation to try and account for so strange a phenomenon as this; and the more the subject is studied, so much the more forcibly the truth comes out that men are not made to be tossed about by the vagaries or the mere opinions of the moment, but require some stable solid help in the paramount matters of eternity. Take two typical specimens of the result of Catholicism on the philosophic mind. Take a leading American and a leading Englishman.

Dr. Brownson, in his "Convert," speaks thus: "I have been, during thirteen years of my Catholic life, constantly engaged in the study of the Church and her doctrines, and especially in their relations to philosophy, or natural reason. I have had occasion to examine and defend Catholicity precisely under those points of view which are the most odious to my non-Catholic countrymen and to the Protestant mind generally; but I have never, in a single instance, found a single article, dogma, proposition, or definition of faith, which embarrassed me as a logician, or which I would, so far as my own reason was concerned, have changed, or modified, or in any respect altered from what I found it, even if I had been free to do so. I have never found my reason struggling against the teachings of the Church, or felt it restrained, or myself reduced to a state of mental slavery, I have, as a Catholic, felt and enjoyed a mental freedom, which I never conceived possible while I was a non-Catholic. This is my experience; and, though not worth much, yet in this matter, whereof I have personal knowledge, it is worth something." ("The Convert," chap. xix, p. 313.) "This much only will I add, that, whether I am believed or not, I can say truly that, during the nearly thirteen years of Catholic experience, I have found not the slightest reason to regret the step I took. I have had much to try me, and enough to shake me, if shaken I could be, but I have not had the slightest temptation to doubt, or the slightest inclination to undo what I had done; and have every day found new and stronger reasons to thank Almighty God for His great mercy in bringing me to the knowledge of His Church, and permitting me to enter and live in her communion. I know all that can be said in disparagement of Catholics. I am well versed, perhaps no man more so, in Catholic scandals, but I have not been deceived; I have found all that was promised me, all I looked for. I have found the Church all that her ministers represented her, all my imagination painted her, and infinitely more than I had conceived it possible for her to be. My experience as a Catholic, so far as the Church, her doctrines, her morals, her discipline, her influences are concerned, has been a continued succession of agreeable surprises." (Ibid, chap. xx, p. 316.)

Dr. Newman almost uses the same words; he says:

"From the day I became a Catholic to this day, now close upon thirty years, I have never had a moment's misgiving that the communion of Rome is that Church which the Apostles set up at Pentecost, which alone has 'the adoption of sons, and the glory, and the covenants, and the revealed law, and the service of God, and the promises,' and in which the Anglican communion, whatever its merits and demerits, whatever the great excellence of individuals in it, has, as such, no part. Nor have I ever for a moment hesitated in my conviction since 1845, that it was my clear duty to join that Catholic Church, as I did then join it, which in my own conscience I felt to be divine. Persons and places, incidents and circumstances of life, which belong to my first forty-four years, are deeply lodged in my memory and my affections; moreover, I have had more to try and afflict me in various ways as a Catholic than as an Anglican; but never for a moment have I wished myself back; never have I ceased to thank my Maker for His mercy in enabling me to make the great change, and never has He let me feel forsaken by Him, or in distress, or any kind of religious trouble." (Letter to the Duke of Norfolk," Postscript," p. 149, 4th Edit.)

Such is the testimony of first-class men who were once outside the Church and now are in. Let us now see what a professed unbeliever says of her, as he looks at her merely as a philosopher, without hatred as without love. "My criticisms of Catholicism," says Mr. Mallock, "are not the criticisms of a Catholic, but of a complete outsider —of a literal *sceptic*—who is desirous, in considering the religious condition of our time, to estimate fairly and fully the character and the prospects of the one existing religion that seems still capable either of appealing to or of appeasing it." (*Nineteenth Century*, January, 1879.)

"Looking," he says, "at the Church of Rome from a strictly logical standpoint, it is hard to see how, if we believe in free-will and morality in the face of these modern discoveries, which, as far as they go, show us all life as nothing but a vast machine, it is hard to see how we can consider the Church of Rome as logically in any way wounded or crippled, or in a condition, should occasion offer, to be less active than she was in the days of her most undisputed ascendancy. . . . In other words, with regard to Supernatural Religion, and Catholicism as its one form that still survives unshattered, I conceive that the imagination of the world has been to a great measure paralyzed, but that it may be seen eventually that it never has been in any way convinced, and that nothing is wanting to revive the Roman Church into stronger life than ever, but a craving amongst men for the certainty, the guidance and the consolation that she alone offers them."

Again : " If we would obtain a true view of Catholicism, we must begin by making a clean sweep of all the views that, as outsiders, we have been taught to entertain about her. We must, in the first place, learn to conceive of her as a living, spiritual body, as infallible and as authoritative now as ever she was, with her eyes undimmed and her strength not abated; continuing to grow still as she has continued to grow hitherto; and the growth of the new dogmas that she may from time to time enunciate, we must learn to see are, from her stand-point, signs of life and not signs of corruption. And further, when we come to look into her more closely, we must separate carefully the diverse elements we find in her—her discipline, her pious opinion, her theology, and her religion. Let her be once fairly looked at in this way—looked at not with any prepossession in her favor, but only without prejudice—and thus much, at least, I am firmly convinced of. I am convinced that, if it be once admitted that we belong to a spiritual world, and in that world are free and responsible agents, there will be no new difficulty encountered, either by the reason or by the moral sense, in admitting to the full the supernatural claims of Catholicism. . . Looking simply on the world as it is, on Science as it is, on our Morality as it is, on other religions as they are, and on the Catholic Religion as it professes to be, what I have tried to show is this: that the Catholic Religion is a logical development of our natural moral sense, developed, indeed, under a special spiritual care, but essentially the same thing, with the same negations, the same assertions, the same positive truths, and the same impenetrable mysteries—the difference only being that what was always implied unconsciously is by it recognized and expressed consciously." In a word, as I said in my Introductory Address, when a man once believes in God, if he would remain strictly logical, he must become a Catholic.

Let us stop now for a moment and see how we stand. On the one hand there is the principle of Individual Fancy, on the other hand that of Authority. About seventy-one millions of Christians profess to base their Christianity on the former principle. Now, when studied, this principle is found to be impracticable—first, because the vast majority of mankind are incapable of making any advantageous use of it; secondly, because it is an essential principle of decomposition and chaos; and, thirdly, because, as a matter of fact, those very persons who profess to act by it, in reality, when their conduct is sifted, do nothing of the kind, but, through the sheer force of necessity, are compelled to do in religious affairs what they constantly do in physical and legal, namely, to take the very best opinions they can command, and act on them. Hence it is I do not feel myself competent to defend that Christianity as reasonable which is placed upon so unsatisfactory a basis; and, therefore, I turn to that other principle of Authority, and feel that it is quite possible, indeed a comparatively easy thing, to give sufficient reason to men of good-will for holding that Christianity, fixed upon the adamant basis of Authority, presents to the cautious mind motives enough to induce it to admit that such Christianity is in accordance with the dictates of the soundest reason.

How does this form of Christianity address itself to the mind? It numbers 230 or 250 millions of Christians. It is acknowledged by friend and foe to be by far the most powerful, united, disciplined, and compact, as well as the most elastic society on the face of the earth. It is ruled by one Head, whom all obey, and who is held to be incapable of leading men astray when he acts as "Supreme Teacher of truths necessary for salvation revealed by God." (Fessler's "True and False Infallibility," p. 43.) The whole of this immense mass of mankind, the great majority of Christendom—is harmoniously united in creed, sacraments, and moral teaching, and forms one sublime expression of unity, amidst the endless contradictions of tongues regarding every other question that is mooted on the earth. Its teaching body is composed of thousands of experts, whose lives are dedicated to the study of Religion, and who, together with profound learning, are the inheritors of the venerable traditions of historic Christianity which have come down from Apostolic times. This teaching body, with the Pope as its mouth-piece, claims, and 250 millions of people admit its claim, to a commission from our Saviour to teach the world the true meaning of the Bible and of Tradition, so far as they are necessary for Salvation; and it moreover claims, basing these claims on the distinct promise of Jesus Christ Himself, to be divinely protected from poisoning the world with error, instead of giving it wholesome bread of truth. Such, in the main, are the claims of the Catholic Church, as admitted and acted upon at this very hour by 250 millions of men, in a word, by the vast majority of Christians.

Now, I have already shown, from the teaching of Sir George Lewis and Mr. Gladstone, and, indeed, from common sense, that it is simply impossible, as things are, for the vast majority of mankind to get on without Authority. I have shown that even those who pretend to do without it are compelled to make use of it whether they will or no, and, therefore, it follows that if it be true, as I have shown it to be true, that the vast majority must take their religion on Authority, it follows, I say, if they would be wise and prudent, they would, at all events, take the very best authority, and the surest they could find. "We may, indeed, allow," says Mr. Gladstone, "that when personal inquiry has been thorough, unbiassed and entire, it seems a violation of Natural Laws to say that the inquirer should put it aside in deference to others, even of presumably superior qualifications. . . . But the number of cases in which a man can be sure that his own inquiry fulfills these conditions is comparatively insignificant. Whenever it falls short of fulfilling them, what may be called the subjective specialty of duty disappears; there remains only the paramount law of allegiance to Objective Truth, and that law, commonly dealing with probable evidence, binds us to take not that evidence with which we ourselves have most to do, but that which, whether our own or not, offers the smallest amongst several likelihoods of error." Now, what I have been endeavoring to show is just this, that the Authority of the Catholic Church can reasonably claim for itself to be so constituted as, amongst all the claimants to be teachers of Christianity, to hold the first place to be, in every sense of the word, the highest, and, therefore, the safest and best authority on earth. And since Religion is a matter not only most difficult, but also of the most paramount importance, it follows that no wise and prudent man would content himself with a second-class authority, but, in such a matter of spiritual life and death, he would feel himself in conscience bound to trust himself to the highest and best. Hence, if it be reasonable to be a Christian, and I have already shown it to be so, to be a Christian means, logically, to be a Catholic; for Catholicity is based upon the only reasonable basis on which religion is able, not only to stand, but, even as an universal laborer, to work.

To show you the value of the authority of the Church in matters of Religion, I will simply ask you to study as a sample her method in proclaiming the dogma of Papal Infallibility. Take, first, the elaborate preparation made before such matters were discussed. "The Commission of Direction consisted of five Cardinals, with eight Bishops and a Secretary, the Archbishop of Sardis. Twenty-four consultors were appointed for the Commission of Dogma, nineteen for that of Discipline, twelve for the Commission on Religious Orders, seventeen for the Commission of Foreign Missions and the East, and twenty-six for the Commission of Mixed or Politico-Ecclesiastic Questions. The entire number of Consultors was one hundred and two, of which ten were bishops, sixty-nine secular priests, and twenty-three regulars. Of these one hundred and two, thirty-two were from various stations invited to Rome." ("True Story of the Vatican Council," p. 89.) These learned men labored indefatigably, preparing the questions for discussion in the Council. Now take a view of the opening of the Council, as drawn by one who was present, and you will see at once what an august assembly it was, and how the authority of such a Senate deserved to have immense weight with any thinking and reasonable man. "First the Pope rose," says Cardinal Manning, "and recited the Profession of Faith in a loud voice. After that the Bishop of Fabriano read it from the *Ambo*. Then for two whole hours the Cardinals, Patriarchs, Primates, Archbishops, Bishops and other fathers of the Council made their adhesion to the same by kissing the Gospel at the throne of the Head of the Church. Seven hundred Bishops of the Church from all the world, the representatives of more than thirty nations and of two hundred millions of Christians, made profession with one heart of the same faith in the same form of words. If any one can believe this intellectual unity of faith, which has endured for eighteen hundred years, unchanged through all changes, in all the minuteness of the definitions of Nicea, Constantinople and Trent, to be a simply human and natural fact, his credulity must be great. They who looked on, still more they who shared in that world-wide profession of the baptismal creed of the Christian world, will never forget it." ("True Story," p. 91.)

Now look at the class of men who discussed and settled the question of Infallibility. There were 744 bishops present during the Vatican Council. They represented the religious Catholic sentiment of the entire globe. Men of high culture, experts in their own profession, and of pure spotless lives, they represent, I think I may safely say, the highest court of religious thought and culture that is to be found on the face of the world. Allow me, in order to bring before you an idea of the representative character of that great Christian Assembly, to mention some of the countries from which they came. Besides 49 cardinals and 11 patriarchs, there were, as representing Europe alone, 40 bishops from Austria and Hungary, 34 from Great Britain and Ireland, 78 from France, 10 from Prussia, 12 from Bavaria and Belgium, 9 from Holland and Greece, 160 from Italy, 42 from Spain and Portugal, 6 from Switzerland, and 10 from Turkey. Asia was represented by 3 from Levant, 15 from India, 16 from China and Japan. Then of the Oriental Rite, there were 14 Armenian bishops, 2 Greco-Roumenian, 1 Greco-Routhenian, 1 Greco-Bulgarian, 8 Greek-Melchite, 5 Syrian, 10 Syro-Chaldean, 4 Syro-Maronite, and 1 Coptic. Africa was represented by 15 prelates, North America by 82, South America by 28, Australia by 8, New Zealand, the Philippine Isles, and Oceanica by 7, besides 53 prelates who had either retired from sees, or had been elevated to the Episcopate on account of their distinguished learning and ability.

"Tuesday, the 18th of July, was fixed for the Public Session. When the definition of Infallibility was proclaimed, it was held with all the usual solemnities, Pius the Ninth presiding in person. After the Solemn Mass, the Holy Scriptures were placed open upon the lectern on the high altar, the *Veni Creator* was sung as usual. The Bishop of Fabriano then read the Decree *De Romano Pontifice* from the *ambo*, and the under-secretary of the Council called on every Father of the Council by name to vote. Each, as his name was called, took off his mitre, rose from his seat, and voted. There were present 535, of these 533 voted *Placet*, 2 only voted *Non Placet*. The scrutators and the secretary of the Council, having counted up the votes, went up to the throne, and declared that all the Fathers present, two only excepted, had voted for the decree. The Pontiff then confirmed the decree in the usual words." The Cardinal continues: "The two Bishops who voted on that day against the decree, as soon as Pius the Ninth had confirmed it, at once submitted and made a profession of their faith." ("True Story," p. 143-4.) And I may add that every Bishop in the Church at the present moment adheres most firmly to that decision, coming as it does, even humanly speaking, from the highest religious authority on earth. The Definition runs as follows: "Faithfully adhering to the tradition received from the beginning of the Christian Faith, for the glory of God our Saviour, the exaltation of the Catholic Religion, and the salvation of Christian people, the Sacred Council approving. We teach and define that it is a dogma divinely revealed, that the Roman Pontiff, when he speaks *ex cathedra*, that is, when in discharge of the office of Pastor and Doctor of all Christians by virtue of his Supreme Apostolic authority, he defines a doctrine regarding faith or morals to be held by the Universal Church, by the divine assistance promised to him in blessed Peter, is possessed of that infallibility with which the Divine Redeemer willed that His Church should be endowed for defining doctrine regarding faith or morals; and that therefore such definitions are irreformable." ("First Dogmatic Constit.," chap. iv.)

Nor is this submission to the highest authority on earth slavery, but freedom. Those who have patiently and candidly, moved by the high authority of the living teaching Church, studied the arguments on which the authority rests, like Dr. Newman, Mr. Mallock and Dr. Brownson, have seen how submission leads to true and genuine freedom. "In submitting to the Church," says Dr. Brownson, "I yielded to the highest reason; and my submission was intelligent, not an act discarding reason, but an act of reason itself in the full possession and free exercise of her highest powers. No act of belief is, or can be, more reasonable; and, in performing it, I kept faithfully to the resolution I made on leaving Presbyterianism, that henceforth I would be true to my own reason, and maintain the rights and dignity of my own manhood. No man can accuse me of not having done it. I never performed a more reasonable, a more manly act, or one more in accordance with the rights and dignity of human nature, though not done save by Divine grace moving and assisting thereto, than when I kneeled to the Bishop of Boston, and asked him to hear my confession and reconcile me to the Church, or when I read my abjuration and publicly confessed the Catholic faith; for the basis of all true nobility of soul is Christian humility, and nothing is more manly than submission to God, or more reasonable than to believe God's word on His own authority." ("The Convert," p. 310.)

To sum up. What has been my reasoning? It is so simple that a child can understand it, and so conclusive that, if you wish, I do not perceive how you can evade it. It is this: The vast majority of mankind must, *nolens volens*, and actually do—even those who call it slavery—take their Religion on Authority. Now, Religion is a concern of supreme importance that cannot be trifled with; but in matters of supreme importance a man is bound in conscience to seek not any, but the best, and safest advice, and to be guided by the highest authority. Now, it has been shown that in matters of religion the Catholic Church represents, unapproachably, the safest and highest authority; therefore it is a duty, and *a fortiori*, reasonable, to be guided by the authority of the Catholic Church. And this comes out all the stronger from the fact that men of profound learning and diamond-like sharpness of intellect, who have carefully studied her claims and embraced her teaching *after having had many years' experience of her*, have found that that authority to which they submitted themselves proved itself worthy of their reasonable obedience, gave them all and more than they expected, and satisfied not merely their hearts, but the demands of their intellects and their most jealous love and mental liberty. Her vastness, her unity, her discipline, her past elastic vigor, her present energetic life, her army of experts, and her historical *prestige*, not to speak of her supernatural endowments, place her alone in the world, beyond all rivalry, and sole and sovereign in her claim upon the submission as well as the reverence of mankind. I said, at the outset of these arguments, that I was addressing the audience before me; and now I ask: What prudent and serious man would dare to thrust on one side the doctrinal decisions of the Sovereign Teacher of 250 millions of his fellow-Christians, and say to me: "Not those, but these, these ideas of mine are God's everlasting truth!"

Who could fairly tax anyone here with being unreasonable if he said: "I am safer in following the highest and most august authority on earth rather than my own private bias on these difficult questions of Religion. I must follow *some* authority; I choose that which is accepted by the vast majority of Christians, and which has earned for itself the most distinguished name. When my body is dangerously sick, I am not at rest till I have got the very best advice, cost what it will. Why should I be less prudent in matters of my soul?"

I hope, then, that I have now given sufficient cause for men of good will to hold that it is reasonable to be a Catholic; and, if it is reasonable to be a Catholic, it is reasonable to be a Christian; for every Catholic is a Christian, though every Christian, using the word popularly, may not be a Catholic.

Thus far reason itself carries us along. But reason, however keen, will not make a man walk to God. We may be ever so intellectually convinced, but that will not suffice to move the heart or touch the will. To believe and tremble is one thing; to believe and to do is another. God alone can move men effectually by His grace; for all the logic in the world will not convert one sinner nor make one saint. Our Lord alone can initiate such a work as that. May He give grace to those who possess already the inestimable gift of Faith, to persevere to the very end; and may He bestow on those who have it not that which alone can touch their hearts, and move their feet towards the heavenly vision. Life is short, eternity is long. We have much work to do before the day closes. Are you in fog and mist and uncertainty of the future? Why, then, not at least consult by far the highest spiritual authority on earth? Why delay when you may gain rest and repose in the Home of your Fathers, in the Ark of your salvation? Or, to use the words of Dante—

> Be ye more staid,
> O Christians! Not like feather, by each wind
> Removable; nor think to cleanse yourselves
> In every water. Either Testament,
> The Old and New is yours; and for your Guide
> The Shepherd of the Church. Let this suffice
> To save you.   [Paradiso, Canto V.

I now leave it to you—you who have so kindly and so patiently listened to me these Sundays, to judge for yourselves whether or no I have offered you sufficient cause for coming to the conclusion that Unbelief is shallow, and that Christianity is reasonable. If I have not succeeded in doing so, then the flaw must be in myself, or in you, or, perhaps, in you and me together, for it cannot possibly be in that glorious cause of which I am painfully conscious of having been all along so poor an advocate.

www.ingramcontent.com/pod-product-compliance
Lightning Source LLC
Chambersburg PA
CBHW020244170426
43202CB00008B/220